ENDORSEMENTS

"Give me space and give me grace" is a theme woven throughout this epic story of the life of an extraordinary woman who intimately knows and trusts God. Gail's life, like many, has been mixed with tragedies and triumphs. She loves God, and she loves others in a way that makes the reader want to be a better person. The book explains how. We have extraordinary aha moments that reveal blessings, like gifts waiting to be opened. This book opens up a plethora of ways to use your space for good. I dare you to read it and do likewise.

— Janna Ross, financial advisor,
organizational strategist, and teacher

Gail beautifully and articulately shares her life story, both joys and heartbreaks, on the journey to create the Blessing House. You will be moved to reflect on how God's Word can "translate your human life into life in the Spirit" to ultimately bless others with your experience, wisdom, and possessions. When put into practice, the Blessing House concept *will* change lives.

— Becky Danielson, licensed parent and family educator,
author, speaker, FaithFirstParent.com

Gail encourages the reader to return to the original hospitality of the early Christian church to receive the stranger. She promotes great freedom for each blessing house to look differently, yet each would have the cornerstone of being a space where God can work in people's lives. God uses our dedication of time and spaces for His glory.

— Barb Zeller, devotional writer and prayer leader

No need to rent a football stadium to bring the love of Jesus to a broken world. Simply open your home—no matter how humble it may be. Gail Berger kindly explains how. (Side benefit: kids raised in homes that love and serve tend to end up in happier, more fulfilling careers as adults.)

— Jeannie Burlowski, author of *LAUNCH: How to Get Your Kids Through College Debt-Free and Into Jobs They Love Afterward*

Reading Gail Berger's story in *The Blessing House* will challenge you in every area of your life. Her story grabs your heart and emotions as she describes God's path for her life. Her heart for helping those who are hurting and encouraging them with her selfless love and grace reflects the very heart of God. As you read *The Blessing House*, may you be open to God's call on your life to be a light in the darkness and to welcome others into your home to help them in their time of need. It is also my prayer that churches everywhere will embrace Gail's vision and learn from her story to reach out in love to those in need. Maybe even start a blessing house of their own.

— Rolf Garborg, author of *The Family Blessing*

What a story and an inspiration! This book is not only a story of her life well lived but also an inspiration of what the Blessing House is and an encouragement for all those people who will use this book to do their own blessing house. A neighbor and I have banded together to sponsor a once-a-month coffee in my garage (yes, it is a heated garage in Minnesota). It will be a gathering of people with a common interest who come from different religions.

The Blessing House can be used for a book club or as a study guide for small groups. Lots of things to discuss in these pages.

— Dave Baston, retired executive MacDonald's Corporation

I read Gail's book not once, but twice. The first time I considered it a road map to establishing a blessing house. However, the second reading brought me to thinking it more of a family "recipe," in that like all good recipes, ingredients can be substituted and tweaked to accommodate what you currently have on hand. The best recipe is merely the chronicling of someone's successful adaptation. The result being that one may replicate it and yet still personalize and conform it to their own signature. Success is not accidental; it is hard work and collaboration. The task is obviously worth it. One only needs to visit the Blessing House to feel genuine peace.

— W. L. Bourne, retired corporate retail executive

The BLESSING HOUSE

Making Your Ordinary Home into a Space for Kingdom Ministry

BY GAIL BERGER
WITH PETER KIZILOS

The Blessing House: Making Your Ordinary Home into a Space for Kingdom Ministry

By Gail Berger with Peter Kizilos

To learn more about the Blessing House, visit their website at theblessinghousemn.org.

Cover and Interior Design: Tara Mayberry, TeaberryCreative.com

Editor: Kim Foster

ISBN: 979-8-9869808-0-5 (paperback)
ISBN: 979-8-9869808-1-2 (ebook)

First Printing

Printed in the United States of America

TABLE OF CONTENTS

FOREWORD

I will never forget the day I first met Gail Berger. What impressed me most about that first encounter was her peaceful, joyful presence and commitment to living a Christ-centered life. As founding director of the triennial C. S. Lewis Summer Institute held at Oxford University, I've had countless discussions with people from around the world about the issues that they cared about most deeply. Yet there was something different about the way Gail talked about the integration of her faith and life that I found intriguing. Her quiet enthusiasm and joyful humility inspired me to learn more about her visionary ministry at a placed called the Blessing House.

Sometime during that first conversation, Gail extended an open invitation to come visit the Blessing House. I didn't know if or when our paths would cross again but found myself continuing to reflect on Gail's ministry of hospitality at the Blessing House in the context of my work in establishing the C. S. Lewis Institute at Oxford University, where the spiritual giant and brilliant writer had spent his adult life as a Professor of Medieval Literature, writer, teacher, and scholar. I became increasingly interested in just how closely her mission aligned with the way C. S. Lewis lived his life.

It's one of the things about Lewis that few people know—just how much importance he placed on a virtue that the material world has often commodified and thereby made shallow and superficial. For Lewis, hospitality was not a surface smile or gesture but a pillar of the Christian life. In fact, Lewis put as much stock in the practice of hospitality as he did in his writing and scholarly activities. A little-known story reveals the highly generous nature of what he practiced without preaching. "When the Germans invaded Poland," writes Kevin Drendel, producer of the website and blog *Navigating by Faith*, "Lewis opened up his home to several groups of children forced to evacuate the big cities." Lewis also regularly hosted the legendary literary group, The Inklings, whose members included J. R. R. Tolkien, author of *The Lord of the Rings*. It was clear to me that Gail, like Lewis, understood the practice of hospitality in its deepest, most spiritual sense.

Some years later, I had the opportunity to stop in Victoria, Minnesota, and see the Blessing House for myself. Located on a beautiful spring-fed lake, the building itself was a model of modesty and taste that was clearly designed with the greatest care and respect for its relationship to the site. Gail greeted me with a huge smile at the door and proceeded to give me a guided tour of the Blessing House, which included many stories about the deeper meaning of the design and objects in every room.

In all my travels around the world, I realized during that visit I'd never seen anything like the Blessing House. Gail had somehow tapped into one of the greatest, and most basic, spiritual needs of our time—an informal, welcoming, dedicated place for God to work in people's lives. I was so entranced by the uniqueness of the house, the attention to space and place and detail displayed throughout the house that I insisted on sitting down and having coffee in every room!

That visit was an important reminder to me. As much as we appreciate the hospitality we receive from others, we often regard it as a special gift granted to the few—not as a practice at the very center of what it means to live a Christian life. What impressed me most about my visit to the Blessing House was the sense of welcome emanating from every nook and cranny.

By some miracle, Gail has managed to tell her story and the story of the Blessing House in this book that makes the spiritual blessings of hospitality come alive for readers in a uniquely personal way—yet universally accessible. In any case, Gail's book, *The Blessing House: Making Your Ordinary Home into a Space for Kingdom Ministry*, will inspire countless readers to reflect on the spaces and places in their lives and how they could be used to bless the lives of others with grace, humility, inspiration, and fellowship. There are valuable lessons on every page. As the world emerges from the global pandemic of Covid-19, and the church considers ways to be more relevant and supportive in people's everyday lives, relearning the value and practice of hospitality will be essential to its appeal and growth. Read Gail's book and put its principles into action and you, too, will find joy in the practice of hospitality and enable others to experience the transformational joy that it alone provides.

Stan Mattson
Founding Director of the C. S. Lewis Institute at Oxford University

THE LITTLE BAMBOO TREE

The Little Bamboo Tree grew very tall and very large, and under its spreading branches the villagers came to picnic, seek solace, and celebrate great occasions. Lovers carved their hearts on the bamboo tree. Weddings took place under the bamboo tree. The tree became the center of the whole community. Everyone loved the bamboo tree. But one day there came a man with an axe, and the first thing he did was to begin stripping all its leaves.

And the Little Bamboo Tree said, "Oh, don't strip my leaves. They're so beautiful. They rustle in the wind and make a beautiful noise, and they provide shade."

But the man with the axe said, "Be quiet Little Bamboo Tree, for I have much need of you." And then he began cutting off her branches.

"Oh, no," said the Little Bamboo Tree. "Don't take my branches. They are my strength, and people swing from my branches and birds make their nests there."

"Be quiet, Little Bamboo Tree," said the man, "I have much use of you."

"Do you?" said the Little Bamboo Tree.

And then he began to strip off all her bark.

"Oh," she said, "why must you do this too? That's what holds me together. It's so important. Why are you doing this?"

"Be quiet Little Bamboo Tree," said the man. "I have much need of you." Then he took a very large axe and felled the tree. Next, he began sawing the whole trunk into small pieces.

And the Little Bamboo Tree wept. "You have taken everything beautiful, everything useful, everything of great value to me," she said, "and you have left me in pieces and without covering."

Then came the worst. The man gouged out the inner core and left the little tree empty of all life.

As she wept with the loss of everything she held dear, she heard him say, "Be quiet Little Bamboo Tree for I have much need of you."

Then he loaded all the pieces onto a cart and took them up the mountain, where he now rearranged the pieces of the Little Bamboo Tree into a channel through which the river could flow down to the village. And there a grove of Little Bamboo Trees grew tall and strong.

PREFACE

EVERY HOUSE A BLESSING HOUSE

"Blessed is the man
Who walks not in the counsel of the ungodly,
Nor stands in the path of sinners,
Nor sits in the seat of the scornful;
But his delight is in the law of the Lord,
And in His law, he meditates day and night.
He shall be like a tree
Planted by the rivers of water,
That brings forth its fruit in its season,
Whose leaf also shall not wither;
And whatever he does shall prosper."
(PSALM 1:1–3, NKJV)

Every book has a story—a tale of how and why it came to be—and this one is no exception. Like the Blessing House, it, too, is a mystery still unfolding. In the telling of it, however, I have gained fresh insights behind this book that can be passed along to others. What I've tried to do is shed some light on how my story and the story of the Blessing House are entwined. It is my hope this may inspire you to look at your life through a similar lens, for out of its twists and turns, your own version of a blessing house will come to life.

The adage "Truth is stranger than fiction" holds true here. To this day, I can't fully account for how the Blessing House came to be. More even than the ground it stands on, the Blessing House is built on the story of my life as it unfolded in the context of God's infinite love and mercy. Since His ways are always mysterious and knowledge of ourselves limited, the tale can never be completely understood. I can describe the chain of events in the material world that made it possible. But I can only wonder at the narrative's perfect orchestration, the uncanny twists and turns that overcame all obstacles and the mysterious power that brought all the pieces together.

The book emerged from countless hours of reflection, meditation, and conversation with my coauthor, Peter Kizilos. Uncertain of how to begin such a project, God provided a man who stopped in to have coffee with an old friend. After giving him a tour and hearing his reflections of the rooms, he said, "I don't think I am here to have coffee but to help you write this book."

The tale of my life is worth telling for a reason—to help you discover the blessing house within yourself. It reveals ways of perceiving events, such as living in the moment, openness to new people and ideas, persistence in pursuing a path not always clear, and especially the patience to know that nothing is ever wasted. Even when it seems like nothing is happening, God is supplying you with valuable, though not necessarily pleasant, lessons essential to growth as both a material and spiritual being capable of blessing others and the world. God is always doing something *with* us even when we feel alone. Learning to trust in the evidence of things not seen requires *practice* in the art of being still enough to see, hear, and feel it.

All of us are born into a world of stories not of our own making that tell us who we are and what to value. Whether our history feels confining or comfortable, we are shaped and molded by things that happened in our past. In the purely material realm, there is no escaping the size and shape of the world we inherited from others.

Yet, that is not the whole story. We are endowed with free will to make choices. We are not simply the product of nature and nurture, but daughters and sons of a God whose world is bigger than our five senses can ever experience.

Neither books nor houses nor people arise by accident. If one digs deeply enough, he or she will find countless backstories linked together and more complex than the life of any single one of us. Strange as it may be, the genesis of this writing reflects in miniature the fundamental faith, principles, and values that gave birth to the Blessing House. The separate and distinct strands of both my life and the house arranged themselves from complicated events that bound them together to display God's power.

God's ways are best told through the language of stories. The greatest blessing is knowing that your own story is rooted in another realm so that your life has meaning and purpose. To know you are living the life you are supposed to live brings both great joy and great humility.

The Author of life itself operates in ways that even the most brilliant among us cannot fully comprehend. A blessing house becomes a window that helps us see the world through God's eyes and experience the miraculous difference that makes. As I approach my eighth decade, I see patterns in life emerging as never before. "Life can only be understood by looking backward," the great philosopher Soren Kierkegaard once wrote, "but it must be lived looking forward."[1] The meaning of past situations and events, overlooked or ignored at the time, often become much clearer in hindsight. We all have a special purpose, some special gift, talent, or way of being that we've been placed on earth to fulfill. The greatest blessing of all is to know and live our own story.

"Now faith is the substance of things hoped for, the evidence of things not seen."
HEBREWS 11:1 (NKJV)

May your blessing house be the evidence of things not seen.

1 David Bouchier-Hayes, "Life can only be understood by looking backward; but it must be lived looking forward" —Soren Kierkegaard (1813–1855). *Irish Journal of Medical Science* 174, no. 1 (2005): https://doi.org/10.1007/BF03168511.

INTRODUCTION

SEEING THINGS

"The question is not what you look at, but what you see. It is only necessary to behold the least fact or phenomenon, however familiar, from a point a hair's breadth aside from our habitual path or routine, to be overcome, enchanted by its beauty and significance."[2]

HENRY DAVID THOREAU

Author and naturalist Henry David Thoreau "went to the woods" near Walden Pond for the purpose of learning "to live deliberately, to front only the essential facts of life, and see if I could not learn what it had to teach, and not, when I came to

2 Henry David Thoreau, *A Year in Thoreau's Journal: 1851* (London: Penguin Classics, 1993).

die, discover that I had not lived."[3] The space and time afforded by his famous experiment in living gave him time to pause and reflect on the meaning of his life from multiple angles. The colors of Walden Pond were always shifting—blue at one time and green at another. He wrote, "Viewed from a hilltop, the pond reflects the color of the sky; but near at hand it is of a yellowish tint next to the shore where you can see the sand, then a light green, which gradually deepens to a uniform dark green in the body of the pond."[4] Thoreau caught a brief glimpse of nature's most obvious, yet hidden, secret: the smallness of our perspective on God's creation. Even a hair's breadth change in our outlook opens the door to an enchanting world of beauty and significance.

The Blessing House is about adding that kind of color and depth to your life and faith by viewing from an eternal perspective what you might have previously dismissed as mundane and familiar. This is both an inspiring and hands-on guide to living with fresh perspective on practicing and deepening your faith in the simple, small encounters of everyday life. It does not contain a set of blueprints for the Blessing House in Victoria, Minnesota. That one was built from blessings given me, just as yours will emerge from the blessings you have received. Thus, no two blessing houses ever look alike. Each is a creation, designed by and formed from within the heart and mind of its creator. As each of us is blessed in different ways, so each blessing house will be one of a kind because it will distinctly reflect what is most alive

3 Henry David Thoreau, *Walden; or, Life in the Woods* (Boston: Ticknor and Fields, 1854).
4 Thoreau, *Walden*.

in you. Yet the approach of a blessing house shares these characteristics in common:

1. You are stewarding what you have been given.

2. Your experiences with God have great meaning.

3. Your history, family, education, and work experience are valuable to God.

4. Gifts, talents, and interests will be a joy to share.

5. Sufferings and disappointments hold incredible power for ministry.

6. Core values and dreams are given by God.

Through real-life examples and thought-provoking reflections, this story can make the blessings in your life more accessible to you and your world in specific ways. Insights into your own identity and purpose will emerge as you see visible patterns in your life from an eternal perspective. Your life, as part of an epic story begun before the foundation of the world, is still being written about the mystery of YOU.

Perceiving and sharing a new paradigm of Christian living connect the tangible and intangible, the material and spiritual realms. My story is told to help illustrate in a practical way how these two realms came together in the form of the Blessing House. In following my path, you will also begin to see your own more clearly and discover new ways of expressing that design in a physical form. This book shows you how to live more joyously and abundantly *right now, with what you already have*. Woven throughout the book is a radical new way of thinking about the concepts of ownership and sharing our possessions, which are at the heart of Christianity.

My primary purpose is to inflame your heart's desire to create *your own blessing house, of any shape or size you choose.* I make no assumptions about what your blessing house will look like. One thing I've learned in this life is the need to be open and receptive to changing vision and ideas. The house you initially imagine will go through many changes as insight and wisdom direct. When you find yourself doubting the process, remember, there is no cookie-cutter, one-size-fits-all formula. It's important not to rush but to cultivate patience. It takes time and space for the blessing house within to reveal itself first as you are translating your life from vision into action. For example, it may not even be a whole house at all but a room, your garage, a backyard, or even a camper or shed, and so on. If you ponder the questions and complete the exercises with other blessing house builders, questions and obstacles you encounter can be discussed.

That is as it should be. The building of any blessing house, no matter the shape or size, is first and foremost an *inside job*. It's in building the blessing house *inside yourself* where the crucial work is done. It's a process of deepening your capacity to both receive and give love to yourself, others, and God. We can only bless our world to the extent we've been blessed. While a blessing house can take many material forms, the genuine article is always grounded in the blessing house inside you.

You will play the role of a detective gathering clues and insights into your identity and purpose. As you begin to see patterns in your life visible only from an eternal perspective, you will observe your life as part of an epic story begun before the foundation of the world. It is still being written. God will shed new light as you gain deeper appreciation for the mystery YOU are. Practical tools and guidance to identify those gifts and talents you may have previously overlooked or taken for granted will direct your desire to bless your world. As you become more familiar with the blessing house inside you, you will also be laying its foundation in the material world.

The structure of this book reflects two major themes of God's ways that brought about the Blessing House. The first seven chapters in **Part I: Coming Home to Truth** deal with the challenge of staying true to yourself and to God in times of peril and confronting the lies and illusions that ensnare pilgrims of faith. Whether these obstacles appear large or small, they present opportunities to strengthen the spiritual infrastructure that empowers you to bless the world. **Part II: Creating Spaces for God to Work** deals with the challenge of how God uses the material world to strengthen and support your connection to Him in the spiritual realm.

Each chapter addresses both realities, the material and the spiritual. A blessing house is not merely a mass of bricks and mortar, but a wellspring of spiritual power that God can use to do miracles. You will be introduced to a radical new way of looking at being a Steward as distinguished from the concept of stewardship. I will capitalize the term Steward to emphasize the unique calling by God to this position of honor. Being a Steward means disowning the possessions that weigh down our hearts and finding a more joyful way of life. It is about cultivating the *desire* to hold everything loosely.

Individual chapters build upon each other, organically connected through my life experiences. They encourage you to reflect on the material and spiritual dimensions that make a blessing house more than just a building. Exercises at the end of each chapter encourage you to share your thoughts, feelings, and experiences with family, friends, neighbors, and members of your church. Experience has taught me above all to embrace life's unfathomable mystery as the most powerful way of growing closer to God, others, and myself.

Each chapter revolves around one or more crucial turning points—what I call "change points"—in my life where I explicitly or implicitly came to a crossroads and had to choose which path to take. Only in hindsight was the choice clear: to follow the ways of God leading to the fulfillment of my purpose or give in to the ways of the world and compromise my faith in Scripture. Circumstances surrounding these change points were often difficult or painful. Yet choosing God's path always led to a deeper faith and broader perspective. Turning to Scripture for guidance at such moments, I didn't always like the answers but trusted in their truth. Each time I committed to live by God's Word, whatever the circumstances, I opened myself to the miraculous power of His redemptive love.

Along the way, you are guided and encouraged to identify the major change points in your life and the blessings you've received, thereby deepening your experience of the Christian life and then sharing it with others. The intention is to bring to your awareness God's ways and help as you practice the basic principles of Christianity in everyday life. This challenges you to expand your vision of living out your faith in more consistent, practical terms. Such discovery will lead to recognizing that you are a blessing house.

The format of the book translates an inherently mysterious process into practical, concrete terms anyone can understand and apply in their own lives. God's ways are never fully comprehensible to us. Yet through the medium of story, this book provides clues to their nature and role in spiritual renewal and transformation.

Whatever form the blessings in your life have taken, this book will help you identify ways to share them. The secret to building—and sustaining—a blessing house in any form is grounded in understanding and trusting God's ways of working in your life.

Creating a blessing house is integrating the experience of living in both the spiritual and physical worlds at the same time. It is one way of bridging these two realities as you begin to see new possibilities and create opportunities for you to practice living as an authentic Christian.

Hospitality is approached from a different angle, not as polite adherence to social forms or a playbook of etiquette for proper behavior when entertaining guests, but as something more soul-stirring and profound. It promotes the radical idea that hospitality in its purest form is *phileozeno* (Greek for brotherly love of the stranger), a commandment at the center of the Christian life. The absence of hospitality in this deeper sense is often overlooked and could be a reason for giving up on the church. Adding a coffee shop as a place to gather socially within a church is helpful, but it cannot replace an experience of being invited into a home. To believe in God, we need to experience the love of God directly through the actual lives of people who call themselves believers.

Who am I? How did I get here? Where am I going? These are the most essential questions facing every human being. God answers with more than directions and mandates. Story invites us into His nature, the human nature, and the break between the two, well-known as sin or separation from God. In the New Testament, Jesus communicates the saving ways of God by living His story as the best, most direct way of reaching the heart, thus enabling the Holy Spirit to overcome our natural resistance to following God's ways.

Learning more about the ways of God will help you more clearly discern the major themes of *your* life, hence the path to fulfilling your life's purpose. As the outlines of your history become clearer and more consistently manifested in the material realm, it will become a natural way of living a blessed life, which opens more space for God to work through your life and the lives of others.

Each of us is given a purpose to fulfill. Our stories count; our victories and defeats have meaning because in our tales lies the secret of our purpose. You will discover that what the enemy meant for evil, God will use for your good and His glory.

The sole purpose of sharing my story is to help you discover and more consciously connect the dots in *yours*—to inspire, encourage, and help you see more clearly the ways God has already shaped—and is still shaping—*your* story. The greatest blessing of all is to know and live as the unique person God created you to be, and thus fulfill a purpose you and you alone can do.

God already knows your role in His grand epic, the character He created you to play. The part of the story we were each created to fulfill proceeds in three major movements—creation, the fall, and redemption—constantly reprised throughout our lives. He knows the reason behind every choice you make even when you don't. Follow His ways and you'll see how perfectly the plot and purpose of your story fit into a greater whole.

REFLECTION

My hope is that you will identify and appreciate the blessings God has given *you*. No two blessing houses are alike, inside or out, because each is a product of one's own unique knowledge, skills, experiences, and gifts. Sharing them with others does not deplete your account but returns rich dividends; it's an upward spiral of joyful living knowing that what you give to others is also added unto you. Trust your place in God's eternal story.

By following the basic principles described, you *will* experience greater wholeness and connection to God and other people. It won't happen overnight, and there are sure to be bumps along the way, but you can move more deeply into the mystery of inner peace—that most elusive and priceless way of being.

The thing you crave more than anything else is found in the liberating truths within your story as Scripture becomes real in everyday life.

Christian living that connects the tangible and intangible (the head and the heart) through a home is God's most powerful way of revealing Himself in love. This book is an exhortation and a guide to practice the life of faith in the ancient ways of Christian believers before they built churches. It puts the blessings you receive and give *at the center of your life*, thereby translating your faith into simple, everyday practices you can put into action.

DISCUSSION

What are you hoping to gain by reading this book? Perhaps you're looking for a way to increase your faith. Faith is basically firm persuasion, a conviction based on the knowledge of God and things spiritual. Without a firm foundation in the things of God, you will operate in human responses, which is where you can be defeated.

Here are some Scriptures that will whet your appetite:

- 2 Corinthians 9:8
- Isaiah 65:24
- James 2:18
- 2 Corinthians 4:18
- James 1:2–7

ACTION

1. Make a list of the blessings you have experienced in your life. Remember, blessings can come in strange packages.

2. Now make a list of the blessings you are currently experiencing. Include even the little things. When you experience a blessing, write it out on a small piece of paper and place it in a "blessing jar." Then when you're feeling discouraged, bring out the blessing jar and read the slips of paper. You will be surprised by the reminder of blessings you may have forgotten about.

3. Begin highlighting faith passages in your Bible or recording them in a journal.

PART I

COMING HOME TO TRUTH

CHAPTER ONE

WHAT KIND OF STORY?

"I wonder what sort of a tale we've fallen into?"
—J. R. R. TOLKIEN,
LORD OF THE RINGS: THE TWO TOWERS

During an early morning meditation by Lake Waconia, a still small voice whispered, "What if you give everything back to Me I have ever given you?" I was moving out of my sixties, having lived a rich life of family and personal adventures with both success and loss. What would it be like to live my seventh decade owning nothing, yet possessing all of life? I spent the next year with R. Scott Rodin's book, *Stewards in the Kingdom: A Theology of Life in All Its Fullness*. May 2008, my church, Waterbrooke Community Fellowship (now Waterbrooke Fellowship Church), decided to sell four of their thirteen acres on Lake Wassermann in Victoria, Minnesota, to fund a paved parking lot. Already zoned for ministry and located in a lovely small town, it was a perfect setting to create a homeplace for God to work in people's lives. This unexpected windfall was the perfect time to take the leap into my new life as a Steward and not an owner, a story all its own.

There was no shortage of second opinions on my contemplated course of action—or state of mind! Many thought it irresponsible and reckless to give everything away, holding nothing back. Some thought it sounded crazy to leave my beautiful life on Lake Waconia.

Some days, I thought maybe they were right. Maybe responding to that whispered call was a bit questionable. Who does that—who gives away all the material things they cling to for safety and security in this world? The answer came swiftly: Nobody. Nobody does that! What made me think I could do that? (Read 2 Corinthians 9:6–15.)

The morning after signing the papers to purchase the site, I simply needed to stand on the land where the Holy Spirit had led me. I knew a lot about this property, having written a book about the history of the German immigrant family who farmed it and kept it safe for more than a hundred years. Our congregation was only able to purchase the farm because of a miracle survival story. A member of our church had escaped the collapse of the second Twin Tower on September 11, 2001, and in thanksgiving to God for his life, his family bought the thirteen-acre farm and donated it to the congregation, thus making it possible for us to build on that site.

I'd never really lingered long enough to probe the land's character, take its pulse, and marvel at its mysteries. Now, it was time to get acquainted, to feel the firmness of those four acres beneath my feet, breathe in the fragrance of the field of purple alfalfa, and walk through the misty bog, listening for the beat of its heart. It was high time we became friends. It was a moment to ponder the mysterious plan that led me here. What kind of story was I stepping into?

The vivid images, the richly detailed grandeur of that day's mystical encounter with the future site of the Blessing House is ingrained in memory. Standing on a high point, my back to the public boat landing, with a clear, blue, aspen sky hovering above me, I marveled at the purple blanket of alfalfa covering the rolling land below. In the Bible, purple is associated with riches, honor, and royalty. Perhaps the sea of purple was a sign, an omen of blessing, a confirmation that this was, indeed, a noble site of healing and restoration.

Looking west through the tree line, I glimpsed the four acres and the gurgling brook springing from Lake Wassermann on its way through miles of swamps and small lakes, finally emptying into Halstead Bay in nearby Excelsior. The only harsh line on the landscape was County Road 43, otherwise known as Church Lake Road Boulevard, bordering the north edge of the alfalfa field.

As I stepped onto the turf that morning—the first time as its owner-Steward—the weather was calm and sunny. Except for the muted songs of chirping birds, frogs and crickets playing in the background, the air was quiet and still.

As I made my first tentative steps into the sea of purple flowers, raising my arms in thanksgiving, a sudden, unexpected wind swelled up, sending the whole field of flowers swirling in a wild, joyful dance. Just as quickly, the wind swept through the bog, ruffling the leaves on the trees, quick to join the hilarious dance. All at once a surprised flock of blackbirds joined the dance, swirling up and swooping across the sky, adding a joyful chorus to this mad reverie of sound and motion.

Surprised and thrilled at this impromptu burst of movement, I was no longer a passive witness to the drama, but an actor hurtling toward a center stage knee-deep in living history. There was no rhyme or reason guiding my movements, just the pure joy of living in the moment. I reached the banks of the creek and looked back over the dancing, swirling stalks of purple. The branches and leaves bordering the bog joined the fray with the beat of the wind. Music filled the air and I heard myself shout: "The land is joyful to know we are bringing the Blessing House to live here!"

Any passing motorists would have seen a strange sight—a woman dancing in the wind, alternately laughing, singing, overflowing with joy. But glimpses into God's mysterious ways are always baffling looked at from the outside. If we are open to those otherworldly ways, we can expect to see some strange sights, incomprehensible to eyes whose vision is limited to the world of matter.

Suddenly, the wind died as quickly as it began, the trees and the leaves and the birds went silent. Peace and quiet filled the void, and the question came again.

What kind of tale have I fallen into?

Flooded with tears, I sank to my knees in awe. It seemed that the whole world was celebrating. The Blessing House would be built here!

Was it all a dream or was this grand affirmation real? Determined to find out, I walked the land every day for thirty days, back and forth and all around, my arms held out in blessing and song. Some days were spent treading the path through the bog along the lake, worn smooth by the padded hoofs of deer who nestled under groves of green branches and berries, their bodies forming soft indentations where they slept. Following their narrow path, I listened quietly for the heartbeat of the Lord and sometimes felt the rhythm of my steps shifting to match the beat of His creation.

I imagined being on another planet, full of mystery and intrigue. It reminded me of hiking in the north woods with my grandchildren, slowly creeping into wild places, creating stories as we went. No rushing, no shouting, only animal sounds allowed. We walked in the knowledge that these woods were sacred, and we but transient witnesses to their mystery. I also recalled travels through Scotland, where I experienced the mystical magic of "thin places," the Celtic Christian concept of borderlands where the boundaries of spirit and matter break down and blend together. This surely was a perfect place to build a Blessing House.

In retrospect, what I experienced those days on the site where the Blessing House now stands confirmed the decision that reasoning alone would never have reached. This was, indeed, a sacred site, a portal to a deeper dimension of existence that could be shared with others. God had stamped His approval. *What kind of story was I walking into?* Certainly one told by the Author of the greatest story ever written.

I remembered this experience as I stood overlooking a crowded auditorium, having finished our fifth annual fall fundraising event. I challenged them to consider how each of their homes was also ordained to serve God's purposes in their neighborhoods. Thousands of people have experienced the Blessing House as an inspiring setting for meeting with friends, families, trainings, business and church counsels, schools, and ministries, along with the gathering of small groups, college students, and individuals seeking retreat. But there was one thing that concerned me.

For all the enthusiasm, interest, and support, I was disappointed that the concept had not caught on fire so that other blessing houses were developing. I asked the Lord, "What more can I do to inspire folks to consider themselves and their homes a blessing in their neighborhoods?" The response came: "I just need someone to plant the seed." I had shown my world the extraordinary lifestyle that brings great joy, hope, and promise to a world worn thin from life. I saw people's imagination stirred, but evidently more was needed to change lifestyles.

This book is the seed I want to plant in the soil of hearts. With the full story of how the Blessing House was created out of my life, I believe Christians will realize how it is possible for them to use their homes for the glory of God. The center of this divine project is to show forth the love of God for whomever God brings to the door—some from next door, our churches, schools, businesses, organizations, and families. They come from all ages, backgrounds, cultures, and all find welcome. Our homes are an embodiment of our lives and can be a living expression of the love of God. For surely that love must be experienced firsthand or not at all.

REFLECTION

What is a house beyond a mass of bricks and glass, wood, stone, and steel? Because we live in the visible world of material objects, we tend to associate the word "house" with the physical spaces and places in which we live. "Home" has slightly different connotations, evoking our sentimental attachments to that place.

"Home Sweet Home" captures that feeling of belonging, of being in the right place at the right time. Home is the stage where the scenes of daily life play out, a specific place that helps shape who we are and may become.

Home is the universal metaphor for connection to the center of our being. We say, "Home is where the heart is"—to which may be added, "Heart is where the home is." It's a reciprocal relationship where one feeds the other. Though it may be hard to describe, we know home is something deeper, richer, and invisible to the naked eye. We are people of space and place and dwell within their double meaning—the realms of matter and spirit. But house and home also bear another relationship to each other. The word "dwelling" is perhaps as good as any to describe the spaces and places where matter and spirit merge.

Dwelling also has another meaning—it describes an action, something we do. Dwelling on a subject means to pause, linger, and reflect, to give it extra attention. We dwell in houses or apartments just by being in them. We also inhabit other things close to our hearts— a garage, a painting, a book, a musical instrument, a boat—the object doesn't matter, only the fact of our dwelling. It could be a porch, a treehouse, a backyard, a bog—anywhere and anything you love—that gives you a sense of completeness and alignment with your purpose. A blessing house is just one of countless shapes the connection between head and heart assumes.

DISCUSSION

How have you experienced seeing God at work in your life? Has a dream been planted in your heart? If you feel a stirring in your soul, ask God to clarify it for you. Don't be discouraged if where you dwell isn't grand or fancy. It doesn't need to be to honor God and bless others.

For Christians, all of God's creation are sacred spaces through which flows the beauty, values, graces, and gifts granted from heaven. Have you ever thought of your house or your special place as a site for God to make Himself known, touchable, and available to others? What might happen in our neighborhoods if Christians began to think more deeply and theologically about their relationship to the specific place they live?

We tend to think of church as the only sacred setting in our lives. Yet most of our lives are organized around our secular lifestyle—most of our time spent outside church walls. This split between the sacred and the secular is not only spiritually damaging, but it is a seedbed of hypocrisy and one cause of our culture's cynical view of Christianity. Consider these questions:

1. What gifts, talents, interests, skills, and abilities are *you* already using to bless your world?

2. What are some things you love sharing with others?

3. If you lived in a blessing house today, how would you greet the strangers at your door?

4. Think of times in your life when you've been—or felt like—a stranger. How were you greeted? How did that make you feel?

ACTION

Here are some ways to begin preparing your home.

1. Many people like to dedicate their dwelling place to God with prayer and anointing it with oil. This is a great way to lay the foundation of a blessing house. To learn more about this, I recommend searching YouTube for blessing house prayers.

2. Begin praying for your neighbors. Prayer walk through your neighborhood, calling the Holy Spirit to sweep through the homes.

3. Create a firepit in the front yard with patio chairs and watch people wander over.

4. Meet your neighbors next door first and begin a gathering place.

5. Keep your front door, garage, and walkway open and inviting.

6. Join with a few others in your church to start a small Bible study group and advertise it in your neighborhood...or a book club, cookie baking party, garage sale, or knitting club.

CHAPTER TWO

LITTLE THINGS

"Two little eyes to look to God,
Two little ears to hear His word,
Two little feet to walk His ways,
Two hands to serve Him all my days."
AUTHOR UNKNOWN, "TWO LITTLE EYES"

Much of who we are is rooted in the kind of soil in which we were sown. Families, where the combination of nature and nurture is most powerfully expressed, have the greatest influence on our growth and development. That's where our introduction to the world occurs, where the stories into which we're born begin shaping us for better or worse. Broader social and cultural shifts in the wider world—the unending stream of changes that ripple through our families, neighborhoods, churches, and communities—also play a major role in forming our identity. To gain deeper knowledge and understanding of ourselves, we must include their character-shaping effects, along with the history of the times and places we inhabit. Added to these complex, confusing, and contradictory experiences are the conflicts between our spiritual and material natures. No wonder growing up is hard to do!

As we start delving into our own life and times, we will find clues to the meaning of our lives lurking in strange, out-of-the-way, small places where we never thought to look. Knowledge of these little things ground us more firmly in the particularities of our lives, the unique identities God created us to be and the purposes He intended for us at birth. The Bible places great importance on ancestral origins, the houses from which major figures are descended. The line from which we are descended can shed light on who we are now *and* who God may be calling us to become. The gift of knowing our roots is one of the most precious blessings of all.

The story into which we were born began with our parents and their ancestral origins. Like most married couples, my parents inherited both strengths and weaknesses from their parents and later passed them on to my siblings and me. My parents grew up in very different homes and circumstances, and the interplay of these differences had a major impact on my formative years.

My father, Rev. Henry E. Gaertner, was born the youngest of ten children in the Texas town of Port Arthur in 1914 and grew up in Malone, Texas. His father, Rev. Henry Gaertner, Sr., hailed from a long line of Lutheran ministers stretching back five generations in a small town in Germany from which they emigrated to the United States. Grandfather put great stock in the benefits of education and expected the same of his children. All seven of my father's sisters went into nursing, and all three boys became pastors. Even though there were a lot of expectations, Gaertners laughed, teased, and chatted constantly. Their rollicking family certainly knew how to have fun.

Among the most striking contrasts between father's and mother's families of origin was their outlook on the world and philosophies of life. My mother, Marian Lovekamp, born in 1922, grew up on a farm outside the little town of Arenzville, Illinois, which hasn't changed much today. The eldest of four girls and one boy, mother lived in a much stricter, harsher, and more conventional family amidst a community of German immigrants. Her childhood was more difficult than father's. She grew up with a mother haunted and embittered by the death of her first child. Her mother's cold, stoic exterior was caused by the loss of her stillborn baby and childhood trauma as a victim of a father's unloving sexual abuse. Words mattered but were rarely spoken. Thankfully, my grandfather was a loving man of grace with a ready smile.

My mother's family was in a Lutheran community focused more on obedience to the law, whereas my father's family loved grace. As I grew older and gained more perspective, I developed a much greater appreciation for my mother's strengths and deeper empathy for her struggles. As a result of her childhood and her mother's harsh treatment, she vowed to never spank her children. A psychologist later told her that there is often a "Christ-child" in a family, who receives all the angry abuse of a parent. She was the Christ-child in her family. She remembered as a young girl, barely able to see over a table, looking at the picture of a man hanging on a cross who loved her.

Like many women in her generation, mother was both talented and intelligent but never encouraged to fulfill her potential. Though her formal education ended in business school, she spent most of her life as a homemaker and pastor's wife, but she had a ready mind and loved to study. Mother was the only one of her siblings who left Arenzville. After graduating from high school, she enrolled in a Texas business college to train as a secretary. Later, while living in Hannibal, Missouri, she attended services at the church where Dad was first called to preach after graduating from seminary. Mother's landlady, Leela, introduced her to Pastor Gaertner. My middle name is Leela in honor of a woman I have never met but who helped determine the direction of my life. Dad's character was much like his father-in-law's—warm, demonstrative, and good-natured.

After marrying in 1941, my parents moved to Carlsbad, New Mexico, a small frontier town that hadn't changed much since its founding. However, when Rev. and Mrs. Gaertner arrived, this small, homogenous community was experiencing sudden change caused by a military training camp established by the US Army in 1940. The relatively stagnant population swelled as wave after wave of new soldiers from across the country came for basic training.

I was born on Armistice Day, November 11, 1942, the holiday commemorating the end of World War I with a big parade. Some of my early years are captured in small, black-and-white photos taken of me with soldiers who attended father's church and frequently stayed for dinner. I was the star at these small gatherings; the reconnection with childhood innocence helped the soldiers feel closer to their own families back home.

I grew up in a world much smaller than I live in today. From birth and all through childhood, I lived in small spaces, the only kind a pastor's family could afford. In Carlsbad, we lived in a tiny apartment behind the altar of the small, stone church and relied on improvisation and creativity to bridge the gap between the space we needed and what was available. Our already cramped quarters shrank further when brother Mark was born in 1944. There wasn't any place for a crib, so every night Mark went to sleep in a pulled-out dresser drawer. When Rita came along the next year, the church moved my parents to a tiny one-story slab house where Dad raised and skinned rabbits in the backyard for food.

Besides the soldiers and the rabbits, my earliest memory is making a little house just for me on a blanket in the backyard flanked by a line of cottonwood trees, playing with my favorite dolly. Every night, Mark, Rita, and I clambered up onto a rough, green fabric couch, where mother read stories to us from a big book of fairy tales, which, now tattered, sits on a shelf in my parlor. Ours was a simple life, poor in material possessions but rich in heart.

I was only four, Mark three, and Rita one when we left Carlsbad, too young to retain many vivid impressions. Yet those early years in New Mexico helped spark my lifelong love affair with tiny spaces. One memory has always stuck with me. One evening my parents arranged for a member of the congregation and amateur sound technician to record me singing the lyrics of the children's song, "Two Little Eyes," cited at the beginning of this chapter. The innocence of that simple tune, true to the beating of my four-year-old heart, remains a touchstone to this day. It is the theme song playing in the background of my life, the spiritual DNA encoded in all I do. The plot was set at four years old: "Two little eyes to look to God; two little ears to hear His word; two little feet to walk His ways; two hands to serve Him all my days."

Mother was four months into her final and most difficult pregnancy in 1945 when we moved from Carlsbad to Wichita, Kansas, where my father had accepted a pastoral call from the Lutheran Church of the Redeemer. Because she had gained more weight and felt more exhausted than in previous pregnancies, there was some early concern about complications. Fortunately, the mystery didn't last long; she turned out to be carrying twins! Already weakened by the pregnancy and the care of three children under age four, doctors prescribed bed rest the last few months before her due date. Dad was ordered to farm us out to mother's family in Arenzville for the summer.

On August 16, 1947, she gave birth to twin boys: Byrl, 8 pounds 8 ounces, and Joel, 8 pounds 10 ounces, the two largest babies born in Wichita's recorded history. They earned the front-page news. These new brothers stood out from other babies in an even stranger and unusual way. Not only were they identical twins, rare enough, but they belonged to that rarest of the rare, a subset of identicals known as "mirror twins," whose physical features were exact mirrors of each other. When one of the twins looked at the other, he saw an exact mirror image of himself. They were like one boy with two bodies. Their uniqueness complicated life in unusual ways.

Our small house and budget shrank further still with the addition of two more mouths to feed. It also challenged the stamina of both my parents. Confronted with the overwhelming job of caring for five youngsters under the age of five before she was twenty-five, Mother was helped only by a grandmother in our church who volunteered an afternoon every week. While she watched us and baked cookies, Mother found a skating rink and spent her hours going round and round on the ice. Father gave up night classes working toward a master's degree in history and took a second job as a school bus driver to supplement his meager salary. Both parents struggled just to meet our expanded family's basic needs. With Mother overwhelmed and Father overworked, I became chiefly responsible for helping take care of my siblings.

Much of my early identity revolved around my role and responsibilities in the family. That I was always part of a close-knit group is reflected in family photos, very few of which feature me alone. I recently stumbled across a family portrait taken shortly after the twins were born that uncannily captures my role growing up. Though it was a familiar photograph, something new popped out of the frame on my latest viewing. Neither Mother nor Father, both of whom are lovingly focused on their newborn twins, nor my two siblings are looking directly into the camera. All eyes are distracted by something else. I'm the only one looking straight ahead, and I am the only one standing; the others are seated on the sofa. At the far left of the picture with my hand on father's knee, I am on the periphery of the family grouping. My expression conveys the appearance of one being in charge. I saw my early years clearly reflecting the influence and importance of the relationship with my father, who emphasized responsibility through the saying, "To whom much is given, much is required."

Even as a child, I always had a sense of being both part of and somehow different from the rest of my family. I played the role of caretaker not only to my younger brothers and sister, but also, in some previously unnoticed way, to my parents. Standing at the far left of the photo looking calmly and intently straight ahead, the five-year-old me in the picture somehow knew the role she was to play in the family. While the burden of responsibility undoubtedly shaped my character in many positive ways, it was also one no five-year-old, including me, was well-equipped to handle. Over time, the duties of the job multiplied and weighed heavier and heavier.

In 1949, Mt. Calvary Lutheran called Dad to pastor in Richfield, Minnesota. Our new home, like most houses of that era, was much smaller than the average-size house today, which made managing a household a little easier. While we didn't have a lot of square feet, it didn't feel confining. Houses weren't as packed with excess as so many are today because material goods simply weren't available or were beyond the reach of middle-class families. The notion of jamming stuff that didn't fit under one's own roof into a private storage locker would have been absurd.

Yet the lack of store-bought toys and gadgets was no obstacle to having fun. Though we had one of the first television sets in the neighborhood, there wasn't much to watch—except for *Howdy Doody* at 3:30! We could make a toy out of anything. Cardboard boxes morphed into sleds, tree branches became swords, large snowballs became castles, and a swamp turned into our jungle.

When it was too cold or wet to play outdoors, we found plenty of games inside. My two favorite indoor spaces were the attic and the basement. The former was accessible through a small door in the wall of my upstairs bedroom. Though the ceiling was too low for me to stand up straight, the crates and boxes became a chair and table, a perfect little hideaway for playing house.

The basement became a workshop and stage for composing and rehearsing shows later performed for neighbors at ten cents a ticket. In winter, I'd build a little house for myself out of pillows, blankets, and whatever else was at hand in one of the corners. Near the furnace, I found a metal plate that opened in the wall where ashes from the fireplace upstairs fell and collected; it became a safe deposit box for my treasures. The hidden corners of a basement became hideouts for playing cops and robbers. I was always creating spaces for myself away from the crowd.

My first scrape with sickness and forced confinement came in the summer of 1951. I was nine years old when doctors discovered a hole in my heart and diagnosed it as a heart murmur. I don't remember experiencing any symptoms, but it was a life-threatening condition back then. I didn't require surgery. Instead, my doctor prescribed an extended period of closely monitored rest to give my heart a chance to heal naturally.

I remember all too well the precautions Mother and Father took to keep me from straining my heart. Given my proclivity for action and adventure, the job required constant vigilance. Spontaneous activity of any kind posed a risk to the healing process. So, to spare me the effort of climbing the stairs to bed at night and to keep the closest watch by day, my parents surrendered their first-floor bedroom and moved into the upstairs bedroom I formerly shared with Rita. Even then, I still had to be carried everywhere, including the short distance between their bedroom and the first-floor bathroom. In order to watch the kids play outside, I had to be wrapped in wool blankets to keep from catching cold, even though it was summertime.

Though I couldn't play outside, a surprise was waiting for me inside. Opening my bedroom door one day, Mother walked in with sheets of colored construction paper, small cardboard cartons, paper, crayons, scissors, glue, and other art supplies. My eyes opened wide with possibility. I couldn't go outside into my neighborhood, but I could create my own neighborhood with these gifts. An imaginary world began to take shape with these bits and pieces. A cardboard carton became a house, a school, a church, a store, each inhabited by a cast of colored paper dolls, complete with popsicle-stick spines that made them stand up straight. Each doll had its own little house, furnished with windows and curtains and tables and chairs to sit in. And, of course, everyone had a story.

My friends and family became very interested and began visiting my little town. As they stood around the bed, I regaled them with stories about life in my storybook town. The walls of my little room melted away. Though still cooped up, I was alive and well in my magical cardboard town, cobbled together with tape and glue, and I was free to go anywhere I wanted. That creative outlet turned out to be a godsend. Not only did it change the way I saw my situation and surroundings, but it gave me the tools and materials I needed to create meaning outside the box I was in. I had the time and space—rare luxuries in a busy family of seven—to conceive and manifest my own creative vision, to make up my own stories.

Stories have always held a special place in my heart; some of my best and most exciting adventures have taken place between the covers of books. I loved reading and spent hours curled up inside a book, my imagination running wild in the margins of a single page. I lived in adventure stories that I read late into the night. Books opened new worlds of experience. What would it be like to be lost on an island? Ride a wild horse? Live in a little train caboose in the woods by a pond, chasing rustlers and saving the day?

My love for books and reading has never waned. I'm still an avid reader and a big fan of detective mysteries, particularly those by author Louise Penny. Her novels deal with the complexities of human nature, hidden layers to the characters in her books, yet subtly expressed in the tenor of their voices, passing glances, slight deviations from routine, the exposure of hidden agendas. Their thinking and feeling sides often pass unnoticed by each other like strangers in the night. Just so, our memories and identities are shaped by forgotten words and deeds from the past and are often expressed in our fears, our attitudes, and our responses to life events. We may question why we have such strong responses.

The other artistic medium that brought me inspiration and joy was an old, broken-down upright piano, with many keys missing their ivory. Music has touched my heart more deeply and directly than any other medium and became the wellspring of my love for worship and the life of the church. I have always felt something magical in the transformation of tiny scribbles into soul-stirring sound. In good times and in bad, music has helped me both give and receive love and express praise and thanksgiving to my Creator. Classic hymns, especially, have fed and restored my heart in times of disappointment and discouragement.

Though I didn't know it at the time, I had a natural gift for music and quickly became a proficient pianist. My piano teacher was also the church organist at Mt. Calvary. Mother said, "Just teach her how to play the songs. Forget the theories and scales and practice drills." All my music contained emotion and rhythm but were encased in a steady and predictable four-four time. I could divide a complex piece into boxes and play slow or fast, but always to the beat of a metronome. My life was regulated by the dependable beat of music.

Before moving, my piano teacher taught me to play the organ using all the stops and pedals so I could take her place. By age thirteen, I became the official church organist at Mt. Calvary, which I continued to do throughout high school. I later had the extraordinary opportunity to take pipe organ lessons from Paul Manz, a famous composer-organist who played the pipe organ at a large church in south Minneapolis. Dr. Manz sent his children to Mt. Calvary Elementary, our church school. Dad asked if he would be willing to teach me, but at $30 per half hour, he could only afford ten lessons.

Words and music have much in common. Johann Wolfgang von Goethe is often attributed as describing music as liquid architecture, and architecture as frozen music.[5] A similar analogy applies to literature and music. Words are the building blocks of consciousness, points of access to the soul—small symbols that connect us to everything around us, including and especially our Creator. As a church organist, I understood music as a mode of transcendence and incarnation, opening portals to the Holy Spirit and greater awareness of God's all-powerful redeeming love. It mattered how I played the hymns.

Words and music come together most powerfully in the form of poetry, a form of art that unites the two and has also been a special love throughout my life. I've often turned to poetry to express thoughts, feelings, emotions, and experiences that I find difficult, if not impossible, to convey in any other way. Writing poems spans the gap between the realms of spirit and matter.

The smallness of the world is always coming home to me at the Blessing House. The strange, providential connections with people who walk through the door never cease to amaze me. Recently, an older gentleman attended a planning retreat here for St. Peter's Lutheran Church in Edina, Minnesota. During their lunch break, I stopped in to chat for a few minutes when one of those "small world" encounters occurred. "I'd recognize you anywhere," he said. Though we hadn't seen each other in

---

5 Johann Wolfgang von Goethe, Goodreads, "Quotable Quotes," accessed June 1, 2022, https://www.goodreads.com/quotes/337462-music-is-liquid-architecture-architecture-is-frozen-music.

fifty years, he remembered me from our years of schooling at St. Peter's Lutheran School in Edina.

That started me thinking more about the meaning of my early school years and where this piece of the puzzle might fit in my life. It took extra effort for Dad to drive me back and forth to St. Peter's Lutheran Church about forty-five minutes from our house. It would have been much easier to send me to East Richfield Elementary, the newly built, brick, public school building close enough to walk to down the block. Yet this small Lutheran school's intimate learning environment had exceptional advantages.

Students in first through eighth grade sat side by side in long rows of desks. I spent a lot of time in that small space, where all ages did so many things together. At the back of the classroom was the kitchen, cordoned off by curtains from the main classroom. We always knew what the cooks were preparing by the smells that permeated the room. In front of the curtain, near the kitchen, were long tables where we ate our lunch before running out for free recess. With so little space, everyone in the room was inseparably connected to each other and everything that happened at St. Peter's. Because the nature of such a classroom provided lots of open time, we spent many hours memorizing the verses of Luther's Large Catechism, which have influenced my whole life. My first Sunday school classes at Mt. Calvary Lutheran were also held in a small basement kitchen, where I fell in love with my teacher, Mrs. Ogden. I became entranced by everything having to do with school and learning. No wonder I later decided to become a teacher!

For the sake of convenience, and the possibility that the change would do me good, I gave the neighborhood school a try in sixth grade. Switching from a small, congenial, private, one-room, church-sponsored schoolhouse to a much colder and more impersonal public elementary school turned out to be a big culture shock. For the first time in my life, I felt like a total outsider. Most of my new classmates had gone through elementary school together and had long-established friendships with no room for a new kid. The milieu of the two schools was also vastly different. The atmosphere at St. Peter's was a stark contrast with Richfield Elementary, where I had my first run-ins with bullies and swear words. I was especially hurt when a boy I liked wrote in my autograph book, "What a face! What a figure! Two more legs you'd look like Trigger." I switched back to St. Peter's to finish out seventh and eighth grades. Jarring as it was, my year as a social outcast helped prepare me for bigger crises to come.

REFLECTION

As my heart murmur began to heal, and the forced confinement dragged on, I became more and more restless. It was so against my nature to sit on the sidelines and passively watch the parade of life march past. Knowing my summer confinement was all for a good cause—my health! —didn't make it any easier to accept.

Looking back, I have a more positive, perspective on my captivity that summer. What felt like a trying ordeal at the time turned out to be a blessing in disguise. This brief period of "sitting on the shelf" stimulated a rare kind of growth no amount of conventional education could ever have achieved. The limits

I endured that summer opened vistas of creativity and imagination I never would have dreamed.

DISCUSSION

Over the years I have come to understand the nature of time from God's perspective. We walk in time and space because we live on the earth and are governed by time and space. But being born again means I also live in eternal time and operate on eternal principles. God is always a Now God who knows the end from the beginning. When I remember I am also an "eternal one" with eternal blood running through my spiritual veins, I have all the time in the world to accomplish whatever God has given me to do. God is a Now God, and in His presence all my needs are met. Fear and anxiety have no power, and so creativity and time are released.

1. Do not despair under setbacks, clocks, and calendars. God is always up to something in your life, and you can trust Him to prosper you in all circumstances. Remember eternity isn't a time word, but the lifestyle or life force of God (called *zoe* in Greek). We have *bios* (physical life) and *psychos* (psychological life), but *zoe* is the quality and power of eternal life that is in God.

2. What are some of the special pockets in time or space you often overlook but mysteriously draw your imagination to explore?

3. What theme song or songs do you associate with particularly meaningful times, places, and events in your life?

ACTION

I have discovered that when I am anxious, upset, running on empty, I have stepped out of *zoe* and back into the physical time frame of earth. Can you remember that anxiety and pressure belong to the earth life? It is natural to respond in panic. I must consciously remember I am now an eternal one, even though I walk in time and space. That removes the pressure and allows me to think clearly and creatively. This is how Jesus walked the earth—never in a hurry, never pressured, available to the thought of His Father.

This week, I challenge you to practice the thought of being reborn in the *zoe* of eternity. Keep a record of how it changes the dynamics of your situation. It is one of my favorite gifts of being an eternal one—reborn into the kingdom of God.

CHAPTER THREE

BURIED ALIVE

"Truly, truly, I say to you, unless a grain of wheat falls into the earth and dies, it remains by itself, alone; but if it dies, it bears much fruit."
(JOHN 12:24, NASB)

It began with the sights and sounds of a typical spring morning at the Gaertner house. I opened my eyes to bright sunshine streaming through the open window of the upstairs bedroom I shared with my sister, Rita. From below came a soothingly familiar blend of smells—French toast and bacon and freshly baked caramel rolls—as mother bustled about the kitchen preparing breakfast. There was comfort in the recurring rhythms and rituals marking out our days, a steady and predictable time and tempo.

It was a spring Saturday morning, which meant the five of us kids had chores inside and out to do before we could play.

We could never figure out why Dad loved the garden when it was only hard work for us pulling all those nasty weeds. Being a pastor now, I get it. Weeding is much easier in the dirt than in people's lives.

Sooner or later our playmates would gather across the street, waiting for us to finish our assigned tasks. They had a stake in how fast we could work because we five Gaertner kids composed a critical mass, which determined what everyone could play—red rover, kickball, or baseball. Mother had a rule about chatter lest we got distracted from our work. So it was a silent vigil on the other side of the street, as we kept our heads down and mouths shut while we worked.

After passing Mother's inspection, we could leave. Meanwhile, the kids hunkered down across the street and listened keenly for the slamming of the kitchen door as we raced outside to play. We enjoyed a world teeming with adventure. Crows and cornfields, swamps full of hiding places, and even the dreaded sticker patches stimulated imaginative play. Steep mounds of dirt and canyons constructed by earthmovers were now perfect stages for acting out scenes from the movies like *The Lone Ranger* and pretending to be Roy Rogers and Dale Evans.

All that was expected and routine. Yet God has a way of throwing in surprises. What began as a typical Saturday at the Gaertner house on May 22, 1953, turned out to be anything but ordinary.

I was more eager than ever to make a beeline for the neighborhood's newest, most popular attraction. A construction company had flattened a hill where an old farmhouse had perched to make room for new housing, leaving behind a very high cliff that conjured untold possibilities in our young minds. We wasted no time setting up our own little construction site on the half-chewed hillside, which soon became an anthill of activity. We didn't have a master plan in mind, but, like little animals, instinctively began burrowing tunnels in the side of the cliff. Caves, hidden from the prying eyes of grown-ups, were magical, mysterious places. One never knew what hidden treasures or dangers might have been waiting inside.

We had a lot of freedom to discover and scout things for ourselves back then; parents felt safe letting kids roam through neighborhoods without close supervision. My penchant for adventure and new experiences, coupled with a keen curiosity to find things out for myself, opened many opportunities for fun that also landed me in hot water later, both as a teen and adult. Doing new things and entertaining new ideas always required risk; yet fear never stopped me from plunging in. I guess I thought I could do just about anything and, thank God, managed to avoid suffering permanently dire consequences. My life was never dull because I lived out the exciting stories from the books I read and the cowboy movies we watched at Saturday matinees.

That Saturday afternoon as we hurried out the door to play at the hillside construction site, life was good; the world was beautiful. I had everything I wanted or needed. I entered the tunnel on hands and knees to resume clawing and scraping out my tiny home. I'd figured out an efficient way to clear the loose soil from the cave. I spread my red skirt on the ground to capture the dirt as it fell. When the pile got big enough, I wormed my way backward through the tunnel, dumped it outside the entrance, and crawled back in to repeat the process. It was exciting to watch the little room grow wider and deeper by the day. What none of us realized, of course, was that the faster our little earthworks grew, the more dirt we emptied out, the closer we came to digging our own graves.

On the last of those many trips backing out of the tunnel, the ceiling of my little cave collapsed and became a tomb. At least a half-ton of paralyzing hillside buried me. Completely submerged in the earth, no one could see or hear me and, for all I knew, even saw what had happened. I was trapped like a little animal, planted like a seed, helpless as an embryo encased in its mother's womb. I immediately tried to lift up but couldn't budge. My hands cupped my mouth and nose in my crawl position and a strange peace came over me. Before passing out, I prayed a simple, silent prayer: *God, please make me an angel.* I knew I was going to die but felt no fear, instead, a calming peaceful presence. There was someone with me; I was not alone.

As I lay unconscious underground, many of the other kids standing near the tunnel entrance were covered in dirt up to their waists, knees, and ankles. Some ran home yelling "Cave-in!" at the top of their lungs. Fortunately, it was a Saturday when mothers and fathers, working on their new lawns and gardens, heard the alarm. Wielding hoes and shovels, they rushed to the site and began frantically digging to free us before our oxygen ran out. It truly was a race against the clock, and every second counted. Meanwhile, unbeknownst to me, two other boys were also fighting for their lives. Johnny, buried even deeper in one of the tiny rooms burrowed in the hillside, was the hardest to find and took the longest to extract. The other boy, Jimmy, was also waiting to be found.

Amidst all the chaos and confusion, nobody knew how many were buried or *exactly* where to begin digging. Men had to work quickly, yet with exceeding caution, as we were running out of air and the blade of a shovel or prongs of a rake could deal a deadly blow. Soon, one of the men struck something hard. A shout went up, followed by a mad rush to clear the dirt. The blade had hit my rear end, which my little brother Mark recognized by the color of my red skirt. Rescuers hauled me out unconscious, barely breathing, just as the ambulance arrived to rush me to the hospital. I came to in the emergency room, where doctors kept me under observation for several hours before sending me home. Except for a few bruises from the shovel blade, I suffered no permanent physical damage. Fortunately, the two other boys also made it out in time.

The front-page story of the next day's *Minneapolis Star and Tribune,* "3 Children Saved After Cave-in Piles Half Ton of Dirt on Them," recorded the basic facts—the who, what, when, and where—of the harrowing drama the day before. The reporter, who interviewed me at home, described the helplessness my mother and I both felt waiting for rescuers to find me.

"There's nothing I could do," she said.

"I was in the same boat," I said, "too scared to think of anything."

The *Minneapolis Star and Tribune* article featured a front-page photo of me lying on our living room couch with my sister looking at me. It was an implicit warning to parents and other children who might be tempted to dig into hillsides. That fall, I went on my first speaking tour as several teachers asked me to tell my cautionary tale to their classes. One question the article didn't ask and couldn't answer was *Why?* Why do such tragedies occur? Why does God allow such things to happen? The struggle to find meaning or redemption in the death or near-death of a loved one takes time to unfold. It took a lot of time, faith, and patience for me to gain the least glimmer of understanding, but being in a cave-in became a metaphor of my life.

Also absent from the article was my prayer, *God, please make me an angel*, and the otherworldly peace and calm that followed. Unable to move, with only a handful of air to breathe, I felt no fear of death—only the peace of God's all-powerful, all-loving presence. The Creator of heaven and earth had not abandoned me. Whatever happened next, I knew everything would be okay. From that day forth, I knew that no matter how dark or desperate life might become, God's love would never abandon me. The faith that flowed from that experience became the touchstone, the foundation, of my life. My assignment on earth was not concluded. I had more work to do—at other times, in other places. God was preparing me for things I could never have imagined.

I don't know about the others, but in my case, the mental and emotional aftershocks stuck with me for many years. The medical profession didn't have a name for this kind of injury back then, hence no diagnosis or medicine to prescribe. Not until the mid-1970s, while treating battle-scarred Vietnam veterans for shellshock, did the medical profession recognize post-traumatic stress disorder (PTSD) as a distinct psychological condition.

Fear of small spaces, such as being trapped in a crowded elevator or smothered under blankets, was immediately obvious. Other signs and symptoms surfaced as recurring nightmares where I'd find myself wandering through a tangle of dark, twisting tunnels with railroad tracks, desperately searching for a way out. I'd wake up in a cold sweat, screaming.

From my mid-teens through my mid-twenties, sleep was haunted by other recurring nightmares, one of which always began as an exciting daytime adventure. I'd be outside, hanging up clothes on the lines behind our house in Richfield, when an airplane would land in our backyard. I'd get in and take a seat. But as I was enjoying the ride, the top of the airplane would disengage and fly off as in a storm. The airplane would turn upside down, and all of us passengers had to hang on so we wouldn't fall out of our seats. I would wake up in a cold sweat, still screaming.

The last nightmare of this kind began with the plane ascending skyward, but this time the day turned to night. I looked at the lights below and realized that the plane was hooked by a wire to a skyscraper. Before the top of the plane blew off, I got out of my seat, climbed through the window onto the wing, and slowly walked the tightrope down to the tower. I never knew what the dream meant, but I surely must have learned a new trust in God to bring me through difficult times.

As an adult, the nightmare that haunted me the longest always opened benignly with me shopping for a new dress at Dayton's Oval Room at Southdale Shopping Center, the nation's first indoor shopping mall. I found a few to try on and entered the dressing room, closing the door behind me. When I turned to leave, I found the door had disappeared! I was trapped in the tiny room with no way out. As fear began to choke me, I noticed that a small tunnel had opened in the wall and scrambled in to escape. But as I crawled deeper, the walls began closing in until I abruptly reached a dead end without light.

Once again, I was trapped and always woke up screaming. The nightmare haunted me intermittently throughout my young adulthood into the early years of my first marriage. I couldn't dig myself out of the collapsed cave, stop the airplane nightmare, or escape from the tunnel in the dressing room. Only God could do that as I learned to trust that one day, He would always set me free. Without knowing it, I was entering more deeply into the mysteries of resurrection and eternal life.

I'll never forget the experience of being buried alive, the most primal of all terrors. Though it was one of the most pivotal change points in my life, words fail to describe the full impact of my miraculous survival. My encounter with God in the tomb that day gave me the ability to help dying people and their loved ones say their final goodbyes. To be fully present at the time of death means fully expressing gratitude and appreciation for loved ones before the souls depart. The unconscious little girl who came out of the hole that lovely spring afternoon would never be the same—a blessing for which I am infinitely grateful.

REFLECTION

Birth, death, rebirth—all life is a never-ending mystery. But rarely do we dwell upon the miraculous changing of these "life" seasons. To build your *inner* blessing house requires close attention to these change points, for they are the spiritual building blocks that uphold its authenticity in the material world. The curtain separating the realms of spirit and matter are not as thick as we imagine; we each have one foot on both sides of the curtain.

DISCUSSION

As you begin to imagine and create your blessing house, look for and identify times you felt buried under the weight of circumstance. What helped to dig your way out? What seeds and new beginnings were sown in the aftermath? What changes in your life right now may be calling for a new perspective? Letting go of any hard-and-fast rules or ideas that inhibit your eternal story from manifesting in the present frees the Holy Spirit to guide and shape revisions.

1. Seeds must die for new plants to be born. Can you recall a time in your life when a seed of an idea died but is now being reborn?

2. What part of you feels buried right now? Maybe you've made plans, but they haven't worked out yet. What would it take and what would it mean to dig yourself out? Where does God figure in your plans? He works in the eternal realm—have you connected with that reality?

ACTION

You've read about different change points in my life. Now, start your own list of change points you have experienced. This is a good time to recall tight spots where God has rescued, retrieved, or rewarded you.

Do something symbolic of burying burdens and allowing God to heal and create something new in your life. If you like to garden, plant a seed, and enjoy the beauty of God's creation as it grows into a beautiful plant. If you don't have a green thumb, buy a seedling and watch it grow. Let it be a reminder of God's transforming work in your own life.

CHAPTER FOUR

GIRL WITH CURL

"There was a little girl,
Who had a little curl,
Right in the middle of her forehead.
When she was good,
She was very, very good,
And when she was bad, she was horrid."

HENRY WADSWORTH LONGFELLOW, FROM "JEMIMA"

When I started elementary school, West Richfield was still largely undeveloped, just beginning to attract the more educated and affluent young families that later flocked to the newer and better homes and schools on that side of town. As a result, my siblings and I drew our friends from different pools—theirs lived in the newer, more suburban Richfield, whereas I ran with the much different crowd I'd grown up with in East Richfield.

By the time Rita and the twins started high school, the more affluent west side of town had grown significantly. Most of their high school friends lived in the nicer, newer, larger homes being built for younger families with more money, time, education, and opportunities to influence and control their kids' behavior. I ran with my old neighborhood friends whose working-class parents were exhausted from parenting. My friends, the youngest in their families, had more freedom to run wild. This rougher, more streetwise crowd gave me many more opportunities for mischief-making than my siblings had. For a free-spirited young girl breaking free any way from convention and declaring independence, this world abounded with temptation. One didn't need a crystal ball to see trouble in my future.

The metamorphosis from "very, very good girl" to "bad girl with the curl" took a long time coming. Up until I turned fourteen and was in my freshman year at Richfield High School, I was the dutiful daughter who got good grades, stayed out of trouble, obeyed my parents, and did my chores without complaint. My place in the birth order played into my later rebellion against authority. From age four, when the twins were born, a large share of the responsibility for taking care of my younger siblings fell to me. The latent conflict between rebel and model preacher's kid began grinding at me. I needed to break away from the image of being a good girl to fit in with my friends. I was conflicted about who I was and had a foot in two clashing worlds—the role model and the rebel—but never felt entirely at home in either.

As I entered my teen years, the weight of being Mommy's helper grew heavier, and it became harder to suppress the need to stretch my wings and fly. It was a big relief, therefore, when the twins started school and I finally had some breathing space. I wasn't going to let other people's opinions of me being a preacher's kid stop me from living *my life*. But establishing an independent identity was complicated by the pile of expectations on a preacher's kid to stay in character, which made everybody happy except me! For a time, I tried being the model child and a rebel, but living a double life was exhausting.

That my war for independence took place in 1950s Richfield, one of eleven communities nationwide recognized by *Look* magazine as an all-American city, added to the drama of ordinary adolescent angst. These model communities made up of energetic, purposeful citizens were also being challenged by a youth culture of rebellion. The advent of rock and roll combined with fears of juvenile delinquency, as reflected in Hollywood films featuring motorcycle gangs and rebels without causes, made adults suspect any deviations from the norm. Richfield was no place for nonconformists. As the pastor of a prominent church in that community, my father was a public figure and moral leader and, as such, he, his wife, and children were all expected to be role models, paragons of virtue. So, anything I did reflected on Father's reputation and Mother's social standing.

Looking back, the lack of a socially acceptable way to express my inner daredevil and lifelong love of adventure was a major source of frustration. About a month after turning fifteen and getting my driver's license, an opportunity to cut loose came my way. I was driving the family's Ford station wagon. Some girlfriends and I were headed to the local diner to get some french fries when a car full of boys pulled up beside us. No words were spoken, but when the boy behind the wheel of the other car and I exchanged glances, the challenge was implied and accepted.

So, I revved the engine, put it into gear, and the drag race was on...flying down the road and jumping the railroad tracks. Waiting for us on the other side was the flashing red light of a police car. I think I was a bit too smug about winning the drag race. The unimpressed policeman gave both of us tickets. The night ended with my sister crying that I'd gotten myself into trouble again. I learned my lesson but not a reformed attitude. The only redeeming factor of the story for me was that the Presbyterian pastor sat next to us because his son was stopped for speeding. I wasn't the only preacher's kid in trouble. Though my daredevil days on the road were over, the shame of my courtroom appearance didn't make me change. I remained as stubbornly defiant as ever.

It was a Wednesday night late in October during my sophomore year at Richfield, and there I was, curled up and hiding like a hunted animal between rows of broken cornstalks, dazed and confused. Not exactly where one might expect to find a Lutheran pastor's eldest daughter and church organist, no less, skulking on a school night. It wasn't where I pictured myself either when earlier that evening I hopped in my boyfriend's car, and we headed to an old, abandoned farmhouse surrounded by cornfields. Nor was it the story I'd sold my parents who believed the lie that we were going to study at the library. By that point in my masquerade, I had become a good liar. Had things not gone awry, they'd never have known where I really went—to drink and party with friends.

Emboldened by the success of past deceptions, I felt immune to any consequences. Even though there would be plenty of booze, and my friends and I were underage, the thought of getting caught never crossed my mind. The party's location on the outskirts of town bordering a cornfield was too remote to attract attention, or so we thought. Around midnight we heard police sirens blaring in the distance that soon grew louder as they headed our way. Someone must have called to complain about the noise. We split just as the cops showed up, scattering like the wind in all directions. I stumbled into the cornfield where I stayed, head down, alone and shivering in the cold—confused, drunk, and throwing up. After what seemed an eternity, I looked up at the icy sky wondering where my boyfriend was and why he hadn't come back for me. Eventually, I spotted a flashlight sweeping through the field and heard his voice calling out my name.

It was about 4:00 a.m. when he dropped me off at home. My legs felt wobbly as I got out of the car, my head spinning and my breath reeking. The lights in the living room were glowing as I stumbled toward the front door. *Not a good sign*, I thought. I pictured my mother pacing back and forth mad, worried sick, and planning her "talk."

As the door swung ominously open, I braced for impact. My parents were relieved but stone-faced and silent as they led me to the living room, the site of many previous upbraidings. They sat on the couch while I sat down in the opposite facing chair, wearily thinking to myself, *Great. Here we go again*. I knew the drill by then. The Norman Rockwell-like scene: upset, worried mother and father on the verge of scolding a prodigal daughter for breaking curfew and disappointing them again.

Mother, primed to play the role of prosecutor, broke the silence. Drawing on her excruciatingly accurate, detailed memory, she rattled off a long and impressive list of my prior offenses.

"And you've done this and this and this and this," she said, barely stopping to take a breath.

She went on railing against my apparent indifference to the consequences. Building steam as she neared the end of her indictments, driving each nail into my coffin deeper than the last, she finished with a flourish.

"This is it!" she raged. "The last straw! How could you be so stupid as to think this doesn't hurt you or us?"

There I was, caught red-handed with no credible defense. I should have been mortified by the open-and-shut case, right? Teary-eyed about staining the family name? On my knees begging for forgiveness. Wrong. I wasn't the least bit ashamed, embarrassed, or even sorry. In fact, I didn't feel anything at all. Still reeling from the night's misadventures and the numbing effects of alcohol and exposure to the cold, my only thought was, *Go ahead. Shoot your biggest wad. I can take it.* In fact, I didn't feel a lick of guilt but perfectly justified in breaking free from the role of preacher's kid imposed upon me. I was long past caring about whatever awful images may have gone through my parents' minds when I didn't come home. I wore the chip on my shoulder proudly. Nobody was going to tell me how to live my life. I'd asserted my independence and there was no going back.

Into the silence came...

"Marian, we've forgiven Gail all those things. We don't have any right to hold anything against her." Then, turning to me, he said, "This is the first time you've ever wronged us."

All time stopped as those words sank in. What the reading of the law couldn't do, the gospel broke my heart. God had to redirect the very nature that was instilled in me, that got me into trouble, to His purposes. The gift of "the risk" he endowed me with had been misused out of my own fear and ego. I wanted to belong so badly I risked dangerous attitudes and actions.

The gospel did what no law could accomplish: it exposed my heart and rebellion against a loving family, against God, and against my own good. Dad looked heartbroken as he said, "You better go upstairs. We'll talk about this tomorrow. It's five o'clock in the morning, and we all need sleep."

I sat there in stunned silence, then slowly and deliberately, my feet heavy, climbed the steps and quietly laid down beside my sister. As hot tears coursed down my cheeks, I said, "God, is this what the cross is all about? You aren't holding anything against me? I have made a mess of my life, but if you want the rest, it's yours...not much to work with, but it's all yours." This was the first time in years, I realized, that I wouldn't have to worry about the lies I needed to tell, didn't have to plan the day's excuses, or call others to cover my story. How could I have been the kind of person who would destroy my father's reputation without a twinge of guilt? How did that happen? How could my father forgive to that depth? I fell asleep with that thought.

I knew my life had just changed when I awoke knowing I was a different person, cleansed and clean. Something inside of me had shifted dramatically. I knew the meaning of grace and felt its healing, renewing power flow through me. I could hardly wait to ask for my parents to forgive me and tell them that God had changed me!

Something about my rebellion had always felt hollow. I was haunted by the nagging feeling of skating on thin ice. I hadn't chosen of my own free will to rebel against my parents, but I was reacting machine-like to a backlog of hidden hurts and resentment. In the process, I'd lost touch with the softer, more tender part of myself. My father's blessing changed my life and bore fruit—both in my own family and service to others—which continues to grow and multiply. While far from perfect, my parents got the basics right. Not everyone is so fortunate. Because I felt so loved and supported at home, I now had the courage to stand by my convictions and go against the grain... and I would need that.

At school the next day, of course, the subject of the raid was all the rage. Fellow partyers shared dramatic stories of the punishments they received when they got home. The lucky ones got a tongue-lashing from their parents, some peppered with threats of abuse. Others paid a stiffer price in beatings or being kicked out of the house with the doors locked and bolted behind them and left to shiver in the cold. Of course, everyone was curious about the special hell and damnation meted out to a pastor's kid and hungered for the juicy details.

"We gotta hear your story, Gaertner." They were hoping for a real doozy, at the very least, a tale of righteous wrath and recrimination, a stern and lengthy sermon about the wages of sin preached to a prodigal daughter. The truth didn't sound so cool.

With a lump in my throat, I said, "My mom and dad forgave me." At first, they roared with laughter.

"You must be kidding," they insisted. "Oh yeah, sure, you really got off that easy," they teased. "Now tell us what *really* happened."

But sticking to my story only made things worse. Whether I was lying or telling the truth didn't matter. Not having personally experienced the gift of grace, my account didn't ring true. Given all I'd done to stain my dad's reputation and the value my parents and the community placed on it, they didn't believe he'd be so quick to hand me a clean slate. Only then, amidst their howls of disbelief, did I realize just how much that forgiveness meant.

Friends did not take kindly to my conversion. Once I started openly studying the Scriptures and obeying my parents, the jig was up. They knew something in me had changed, but with no frame of reference to understand it, felt threatened. I was no longer one of them and couldn't be trusted. I became a full-fledged pariah. Thus, I found myself dwelling in a no-man's land my junior year, doubly rejected—by the "bad" kids for being too "good," and the "good" kids for being too "bad." I had no friends in either camp and thought I might spend the rest of high school walking alone. Yet there was no turning back. I was free from living in the dark.

Things mysteriously changed my senior year. Not only was I brought out of exile, but for the first time in my life, I entered the ranks of the popular, more affluent crowd living on the "right side" of the tracks. I dated the sports heroes, participated in plays and musicals, and that fall was voted onto the homecoming court, one of eight girls in a class of eight hundred students.

There's no getting around the hurt of rejection and isolation I felt most of my sophomore and junior years. It wasn't easy having former friends turn away when we saw each other in school, but God sent one special friend to sit with me at lunch. I learned a lot from walking alone. If one is open and receptive to God, no experience is wasted. Later, as a teacher, it served me well in connecting with my students. Because I, too, had strayed from the straight and narrow path, I could empathize and understand; rebellious kids didn't scare me. They trusted me because I'd walked in their shoes, an experience God later used as a power tool for building my teen ministry called Joyful Noise.

I ran several gauntlets that year with my parents, my rowdy friends, the "good" and popular kids, but I came out the other side stronger. With God's grace, I stayed true to the Lord, myself, and my values. I gained greater courage in my new walk with Christ.

After blatantly breaking the rules, my father could have read me the riot act and sentenced me accordingly. Instead, he said, "We don't hold this against you. Your slate is wiped clean. It's as if none of this had happened."

Of his own free will, no strings attached, my dad forgave me. Looking back, that 4:00 a.m. scene in the living room was a major change point in my life. Though I didn't know it then, God was building a foundation for the future Blessing House.

REFLECTION

I knew a lot about the *laws* of God before that night in the cornfield. I was a pastor's daughter, attended church and Sunday school all my life, and was the church organist at Mt. Calvary from age thirteen through high school graduation. But until that night, I had not experienced the *ways* of God. The blessings I got from following the rules were not as life changing as those received when I strayed.

My father's mysterious power of forgiveness intrigued me to the depths of my being. How was such a thing possible? What else might be possible? It was also the beginning of a lifelong identity crisis that raised the most basic questions of existence: Who am I? Who is God? What is my purpose? What values do I hold so strongly that I'll walk alone to uphold?

Forgiveness freed me to be molded by the truth of Scripture without fear of failure. I now understood I could learn and grow from every experience. In fact, my life became a series of change points, each of which brought me closer to God, more aligned with the purpose for which I was created. That was the most profound change point in my life: the grace of forgiveness changed everything. As fruits of that experience filtered deeper and deeper into every fiber of my being, I began trusting God as never before. In fact, this one event enabled me to pass through deep waters of forgiveness on many occasions in my whole life of relationships. I didn't realize that without these foundations taking deep root, my recovery of life events would certainly have been at risk in my future.

I didn't seek to be a rebel; I simply wanted to be accepted by my friends—and God allowed me to experience the dangers of going the ways of the world. The God-given need to belong can become twisted in our deep desire for connection that leads to self-destructive behaviors and hazardous relationships founded on false premises of belonging and worldly success. Learning to discern the difference is the project of a lifetime; it takes a lot of courage and a willingness to risk finding out.

DISCUSSION

Shoehorning ourselves into boxes of any kind, made by others or ourselves, stunts our growth and causes us to slowly wither and die. An open, empty box, on the other hand, is full of possibilities. Observe what small children do with their presents on Christmas morning. They often prefer playing with empty boxes than the gifts that came inside. Their imagination can turn an empty box into anything: a castle, a car, a stage, a train—a place to pour their heart's desire.

1. What boxes you in your world (i.e., concepts, dreams, feelings, attitudes, beliefs)?

2. In what ways do you limit your ability to fulfill your purpose by the language you use? For example: "God doesn't speak to me," or "I'm too old to do this; my mind is forgetful and easily muddled."

3. Can you share a story of when your faith became real to you?

ACTION

1. The following actions can help you see how your faith has matured. Many people believe they had faith when they were children, but somehow they've lost track of it as adults.

2. Wander through the toy section at a local merchant. What toys are you attracted to? What about the box or packaging sparks your imagination? Consider purchasing something small, take it home and play with it for a while, and journal about the experience to bring back childhood delights. Does it bring back an important memory? Is it something you can tell a God-story about?

3. Perhaps the experience brings up a sad or difficult memory. Are you holding something against God that is hazardous to your future adventures? If so, talk to God about it.

CHAPTER FIVE

WHO ARE YOU?

"For you formed my inward parts;
you knitted me together in my mother's womb.
I praise you, for I am fearfully and wonderfully made....
Your eyes saw my unformed substance; in your book were
written, every one of them,
the days that were formed for me, when
as yet there was none of them."
(PSALM 139:13–14A, 16, ESV)

I remember climbing the ladder and stepping out onto the high dive, looking down at the shimmering surface of the Valparaiso Recreation Center's brand-new indoor pool, just a few short blocks from the sorority dorm where I was living. Proximity to the new pool made it easy for me to slip a dip into my schedule. I'd always admired divers and their fearless stunts, especially the backward dive. One day I watched a young man climb several times to the highest deck and make daring leaps backward into the pool, cutting the water like a knife. He made it look so easy.

And now there I was, turning and inching my body backward toward the end of the platform. The excitement of climbing the ladder gave way to fear as I backed my heels off the edge of the board, wondering, *What makes me think I can do this?* But this was no time for second thoughts. I had to focus on jumping high and away to avoid hitting my head on the way down. I had to turn off my mind and trust my feet to take over, to push forward and up. And then...I plunged!

I wasn't prepared for the strange sensation of not seeing the water down below, but only the roof above me as I hurtled head back and down into a pool I couldn't see. My landing wasn't quite as graceful as his. Instead of smoothly piercing the surface of the pool, I hit the water at an awkward angle and felt the shock ripple through my body. Yet my arms and head were pointing down as they should—that was success!

Had I really done a backward dive off the high board—or had I dreamed it up? Did it happen in the real world or only my imagination? To prove to myself that, yes, it really happened, I went back up the ladder and repeated my performance. Twice was enough. Whatever caused me to question myself had worked its way out of my system. There was nothing left to prove.

It takes discernment and spiritual maturity to know what risks are worth taking; are positive; are done from love, not fear; and aren't derived from some egotistical desire to show off or elevate oneself by having taken the risk. It takes a certain knowledge, wisdom, and maturity to know the right time, place, and reason to take such a leap. I knew myself well enough that a backward dive was within the range of possibilities based on my experience. I was born into a loving family that provided a sturdy platform from which to make such choices.

Only you and God know if or when it's time to attempt your version of a backward dive. My risky judgments are now based on (1) past experiences, (2) knowing the difference between self-satisfaction and wanting to satisfy others, (3) acting in love and not fear, and (4) confidence in the time and place to take such a leap.

College was a time of self-discovery for me, as it is for many young people. While I had already developed a strong sense of myself and refined key parts of my character, leaving home stimulated the need and desire to integrate and further build upon the foundation of my identity in the context of the wider world. Did the sum of my parts add up to a greater whole? I didn't have the awareness to ask the question consciously. Looking back, however, that's what I was doing—experimenting, trying things out, taking positive risks that revealed new aspects of the person I was and wanted to become.

"Know thyself," the Greek philosopher, Socrates, wisely advised. Yet that is often more difficult, even dangerous, than one realizes. Socrates was eventually tried for treason and sentenced to death by the Athenian authorities for such truth.

One of the biggest surprises was discovering my brain. I didn't accomplish much academically in high school or see myself as smart. Yet a love of learning had begun surfacing in Miss Baume's history class my senior year. There was a teacher whose passion and enormous body of knowledge about ancient history brought the subject to life and piqued my curiosity about how people lived in the distant past. Though uncomfortably large, Miss Baume was constantly in motion, whizzing about the classroom in her four-wheeled chair, entrancing us with stories of ancient Babylon, Greece, Rome, and Egypt. I was hooked...and still am.

Given my lackluster high school grades, I was pleasantly surprised to discover my intellectual curiosity and passion for academics in college. Surrounded by a rich culture of intellect, high principle, and energy for community life, I felt a surge of excitement in college life and fell in love with learning. The Christian mind is glorious, and the fact that the university was steeped in its elegant values and ideas gave me an unusual joy. The opportunity to engage with high-minded professors, study in magnificent libraries, and meet students from all across the nation was an unexpected blessing. I was diligent in my studies and never fell behind, which also came as a surprise! Most importantly, I fell in love with everything about the Scriptures; it became my obsession. I was stunned by the reality of the Bible's authenticity, reliability, and historicity and somewhat disturbed that I was never taught this.

I also thrived by joining a small group of nineteen other girls to form a new sorority on campus our sophomore year. In the process of founding Kappa Psi Omega, I discovered my passion for joining with other creative minds to pour out ideas and put them into practice. My role in founding the new sorority was a major milestone in my personal and social development. One thing I learned is the world is run by those who simply show up. Even a small, committed group can change the direction of history.

As a member of the pre-baby boom generation, I always found myself on the cusp of change, at the intersection of old ways dying and something new waiting to be born. Valparaiso welcomed the largest class of freshmen to ever hit the school, which meant there was not enough room in the sororities to accommodate the surge of new women wanting to pledge. Necessity became the mother of invention, and I became a charter member of Kappa Psi Omega (now Kappa Kappa Gamma). The twenty of us created an "All American Girl" sorority with new traditions, songs, creeds, emblems, dress, and events. As the chaplain and songster, I developed the spiritual and musical persona of the Kappa sorority.

When I returned to Valparaiso twenty-five years later to meet the "sisters" and hear about the sorority's fame, success, and status at the university, I was the first "founding mother" they had ever met. It was gratifying to see they had stayed true to its mission of producing exceptional women leading successful, Christ-centered lives. In listening to their stories, I was reminded how the fundamentals we installed were still guiding and attracting the smart, beautiful Christian women for whom we created a living space on campus.

Rooming with my friend Linda, a fellow leader of the sorority, our senior year reawakened the passion for exploring new experiences. So, we planned a trip to Europe in the summer of 1965 after graduation and a year of teaching. I wanted to visit all those ancient places Miss Baume had talked about. To afford the trip on our teachers' salaries, we bought the popular guide, *Europe on $5 a Day*, to help us travel on the cheap.

Not everyone shared our enthusiasm. Some judged the notion of two young women, with no travel experience, too risky and naive. Yet we were supremely confident that we could meet the challenge. As to the future, we both planned to teach a few years, get married, buy homes, and raise a family. Like most women of our generation, we didn't question those goals or consider alternatives. To most people, however, we were embarking on a dangerous summer.

I went home during spring break to look for a teaching job that would enable me to gain experience, support myself, and start saving for Europe. Thanks to historical circumstances, it was a great time to be entering my field. A spike in the school-age population resulting from the post-World War II baby boom sent school districts nationwide scrambling to build new schools and hire more teachers. It didn't take long to find and apply for a good fit: an opening for a sixth-grade teacher in the Bloomington public schools. I sent a letter indicating my interest in the position and soon after received a response inviting me to interview.

As I pulled into the school's parking lot the day of the interview, I felt confident and well prepared, certain of possessing the skills, abilities, knowledge, temperament, experience, and passion to be a good teacher. I had gained confidence and experience during my teaching internship in the Valparaiso public schools. Due to the regular teacher's sudden illness, I had the rare opportunity to take complete charge of the class, which felt like an "old shoe."

On entering the interviewer's office, I introduced myself and exchanged a few pleasantries. The man behind the desk seemed friendly and businesslike, and I had no difficulty responding to all the standard questions about my work experience, college coursework, motivation for teaching, future plans, and so on. It was all going smoothly, or so I thought, until the curve ball came.

"I'm going to ask you ten questions," he said, stone-faced, nothing in his voice hinting at the radical new line of questioning he was about to open. A short answer would do, he said, a word or a few sentences at most. If I didn't mind, he added, he'd like to record my responses. *Okay*, I thought, *have at it*.

"Who are you?"

I don't recall if I blinked, cleared my throat, or gave any other indication of being caught off guard by both the blunt and personal nature of the question. Strange as it may seem, no one had ever asked me that most basic and profound question. There were so many possibilities. But from which long list of vital statistics should I choose? The question was intended to elicit something deeper and more revealing than name, rank, and serial number. But at twenty-two, I probably said something like "I'm a teacher."

Well, that was easy, I thought—a perfect job interview response. I tailored my identity to fit the person I thought most likely to be hired. One down, nine to go. If the rest were anything like the first, this was going to be a piece of cake.

Little did I know, the interrogator was just warming up. I found the second question even more startling.

"Who are you?"

Wait a minute. Hadn't I just answered that? He was obviously trying to get at something deeper, but what? That simple question was repeated again and again and kept getting harder to answer. Flustered, I groped for something more impressive and profound to say about myself.

"Well, I'm female." "Uh, I'm a sister." "I'm, um, a traveler." "I'm a reader," "a pianist," I replied, soon exhausting my repertoire of simple selves.

Mercifully, the quiz was almost over. For the tenth and final time, he repeated, "Who are you?"

What else was left? My mind went blank, yet I had to come up with something quick.

"I'm a Christian," I blurted out, almost desperately.

Appearing slightly bemused, the interviewer put down his pen, looked me straight in the eyes and said, "That surprises me. As a pastor's daughter, I would have thought that would be first on your list."

That single comment became a change point. For not only was I born into the faith, but I'd fallen in love with the Scriptures and the world of theology at Valparaiso! How could I have missed the obvious—the centrality of my faith to my identity?

I was as much in the dark as the interviewer.

Not until the interview was over and I was walking back to the car did the weight of the question and its implications sink in. After all, I was a pastor's kid whose heritage on my father's side was a long line of ministers stretching back many generations. I grew up immersed in church life and culture, regularly attended church on Sundays, and from sixth grade through high school was the church organist. I was about to graduate from the nation's largest Lutheran university and even helped start a sorority founded on the mission of developing Christian all-American girls.

The interviewer was right. The fact that "Christian" showed up last on my list *was* puzzling. Who was I and why did I give "Christian" bottom billing? It was not for fear of recrimination or hurting my chance to get the job. In the context of the times, public school teachers freely identified as Christians. I had confessed my faith on far more trying circumstances; in high school, for example, I paid the price of being ostracized and rejected by my peers.

How could I, so deeply immersed in church life and culture from birth, have been so blind to the core of my identity? The truth was that despite the strong faith instilled by my Christian upbringing, background, and experience, I had not consciously and consistently placed Christianity front and center of my identity. I'd taken the existential grounding of my faith for granted. It was the air I breathed, the water I was always swimming in. Christianity wasn't a label but a way of life, a way of being. Looking back, it was the first time I publicly identified myself as Christian—as an identity, not just a group I belonged to or a belief system or a general category of religion.

A few days later, a letter arrived in the mail offering me the job. In the flurry of activity that followed, the question was temporarily forgotten. But it lodged itself somewhere in my consciousness where it continued to fester. Some part of me remained doggedly determined to solve the deeper truth of who I was and wanted to become.

By graduation, I thought I knew myself well. Though my transition from college to a teaching position was relatively smooth, my quest for self-knowledge had barely begun. I landed a good job in my field, confirmed my vocation, and was learning to create a life of my own as an adult. In addition to teaching and actively participating in church, I was meeting new people, making new friends, learning more about myself. The future looked bright.

The first year of teaching was busy with days that didn't end at the bell. There were always lesson plans to prepare, homework assignments to grade, records to keep. Every Thursday night, however, I accompanied the church choir practice. On a Thursday night sometime in January 1965, the director canceled practice due to illness. I took advantage of the rare weeknight opening to go out for a Shakey's pizza with a girlfriend.

In the meantime, Bob Berger, who was sharing a condo with some friends, also broke routine. As a group, they ordinarily went to Shakey's Pizza, the newest hotspot in town on Wednesday nights. But that week, they switched to Thursday. My friend and I were already seated with a beer and pizza when the guys spotted us. They rolled dice, I later learned, to see which of them would make a move on us. Since Bob wasn't one of the winners, he stayed back while a couple other guys approached and struck up a conversation.

After a little small talk, Bob, who had a girl on his arm, came over and introduced himself—then proceeded to focus all his attention on me! He was hooked the minute he found out I was a teacher, his friends told me later. I, on the other hand, didn't like anything about him—like the way he rudely ignored the girl he was with. My first impression wasn't good. I didn't want anything more to do with him.

Before going our separate ways, the guys invited us to a party at their place that Saturday night. They seemed nice enough and it sounded fun, so we accepted. Because it was the first party I'd been invited to since college and didn't know who else might be there, I wanted to make a good impression. At 5′ 2″, I was worried about not getting noticed. So, I came up with an attention-grabbing gimmick: I got my hair cut in a fashionable manner, short on one side, long on the other, and bought myself a long, red cigarette holder. I knew most guys were shy about talking to girls, so I added some style and accouterments as conversation starters.

I noticed Bob scouting me out at the party and deliberately ignored him. Eventually, there was no escape. I was trapped standing in a long line to use the bathroom, and he offered to wait with me. Afterward, he teasingly said I owed him a dance for waiting. We danced. That's all it took. I fell in love dancing in his arms—a perfect fit.

One thing Bob revealed that night was that he loved playing bridge. A couple had been bugging him to find a girl that liked bridge, so I told him I loved to play bridge. There was only one hitch, I didn't know the first thing about the game. My last year of college I lost a boyfriend to bridge, and I wasn't going to let that happen again! I gave him my phone number, and he promised to call. The next day I asked mother for a favor.

"This guy might be calling me, and since I'll be out for the evening, would you please tell him I was at my bridge club?" And she did!

I dived into learning the game, in case he called my bluff. Though I spent my break times at school reading up on the game, my brain had no time to absorb it. When we joined his friends to play bridge, I'd have to fake my way through the evening to avoid detection. By the second round of bidding, Bob could tell I was clueless. Ironically, my lack of knowledge turned out to be a plus. The randomness of my bids so confused the other side that we went home the winners.

As Bob opened the car door, he said chuckling, "You've never played bridge before, have you?" He wasn't irritated but impressed. "Any woman that can get away with what you did tonight is my kind of woman." That risk paid off.

Looking back, I'm surprised at myself. *What made me think I could do that?* It's a question I've pondered all my life. What gave me the confidence to overcome reasonable doubt, to imagine the impossible was possible, and to make such large leaps of faith? If I saw someone else doing it, I seemed sure I could do it too. I believe it was a hunger for life, adventure, expansion, and opportunity.

REFLECTION

"Who are you?" It's the most difficult and pressing issue of any day, the implications of our answers are enormous. The world of matter from which we're made is constantly in flux, never the same yesterday, today, or tomorrow. "One never steps into the same river twice," goes an ancient saying. We, too, are always works in progress. God, on the other hand, knows us chapter and verse—who we are, where we've been, and where He intends us to go. If we stop and listen closely, we will hear Him whispering the way.

DISCUSSION

Before meeting with your group, write down ten, one-word answers to the question, "Who are you?" As you review your answers, what did you discover about yourself?

1. Many people identify themselves as a Christian. On what basis do they say or think they are a Christian?

2. Did you realize that being a Christian isn't a belief system but a core identity?

3. What core identity within you might have to go?

ACTION

If someone were to ask you about being a Christian, would you be able to clearly articulate what it means to be a Christian? Practice writing out your response.

CHAPTER SIX

THE HEARKENING

"But whoso hearkeneth unto me shall dwell safely, and shall be quiet from fear of evil."
(PROVERBS 1:33, KJV)

Like many newlyweds, Bob and I didn't really know each other, or ourselves, all that well before getting married. In fact, we'd met, dated, and fallen in love only a few months before June of 1965, when Linda and I sailed for Europe in search of new, life-expanding experiences. When he offered to drive me to the train station in St. Paul to catch the Empire Builder to Chicago, the first leg in our transatlantic tour, I assumed it was just to say a special *bon voyage*.

It was a quiet ride to the station, but Bob clearly had something on his mind. I chalked it up to his worried anticipation of my impending absence. Standing on the platform, however, the mystery was revealed. Just as I was boarding the train, he asked me to marry him!

Bob had a lot going for him—a promising career teaching business at the University of Minnesota, a brilliant mind, an excellent moral character, even the baby-blue convertible! He was also suave, sophisticated, and a lot of fun. We had a lot in common: we were both leaders, ambitious, sociable, and loved to dance. I felt ready to be married, so I didn't hesitate to accept his proposal. In the few months we dated, we had both fallen hard for one another and could be excused for wanting to secure our relationship before I sailed.

Linda and I, twenty-two-year-old first-year teachers, were both supremely confident that no matter what happened, we were going to savor every minute of our exotic adventure, beginning with a transatlantic voyage on the *S.S. France.*

Once settled on board, we were delighted to find that our dinner table assignment included two lovely, retired ladies who were British professors of English literature and loved quoting poetry for every occasion, often causing uproarious laughter. Also seated were two charming, silver-haired, impeccably mannered French gentlemen who regaled us with stories. Our table of six had scintillating dinner conversations often followed by cocktails in one of the many pubs on the ship. One evening I mentioned my desire to shop for a trousseau in one of the Paris shops but was concerned about the language barrier. One of the Frenchmen offered to help me, and I had the good sense to accept. He agreed to meet me in Paris and help me shop for my honeymoon attire. While shopping, he gave me some good advice.

"Mademoiselle," he said, "you must leave a little bit to the imagination."

After docking in the London port and saying goodbye to our new friends, we hailed a taxi for a wild ride through the streets of London to our hotel. As a big fan of British history and literature, I was especially keen on touring ancient castles and visiting where Shakespeare had lived. Linda loved the museums and city life. After a week treading the English countryside and catching "Camelot" in an ancient London theater, we were off to Paris. The one silver lining to the rocky, stomach-churning flight over the English Channel was a gentleman who worked for the United Nations. He invited us to attend several official soirées hosted by diplomats in the foreign service. Paris was exceptional!

Despite a rainy summer, we were too excited to let that dampen our adventurous spirits. It would take a whole book to chronicle the most dramatic episodes in our travels through England, France, and the mountains of Austria, Germany, Italy, and Switzerland. There was the time we got kicked out of our hotel room in Amsterdam in the middle of the night for inviting a couple of girls with no place to stay to crash with us. An enraged hotel clerk banged on our door at 4:00 a.m., stormed into the room and threw our suitcases out the fourth-story window, scattering our clothes onto the street! Then there was the incident in the English pub when we discovered, much to our chagrin, that we didn't have enough money to pay the bill and had to wash dishes to square our account. In Italy, we had to be especially on guard against flirtatious young men and keep a close eye on our purses anytime we took a bus. Our trip down the Rhine River reached the end of the line at a deserted train station where we spent the night fending off an attendant who strictly enforced the rule of no sleeping in the station.

When the train finally arrived, we immediately fell asleep in our sitting quarters as the train rumbled through the Alps on our way to Venice. I remember lying on the hard, wooden slats with our backpacks for pillows, with the steady rhythm of the train lulling us to sleep, innocent and vulnerable. I felt the palpable presence of a shadow lurking in the darkness. I could hear Linda's soft snoring and the clacking rhythm of the train. I felt a hand on my foot. Half asleep, I changed positions, instinctively pulling my knees up close, yet the chilling hand continued moving up my leg. In a reflex action my foot sprang out and found its mark. I heard a grunt, and the door latch opened and closed. I sat up in a cold sweat. Evil without a face became a reality.

We had our itineraries well planned so our families could keep track of where we were. Letters from Bob made it sound like he was having a grand time, meeting new people (including women), and doing just fine without me. I didn't know what to think at the time—maybe he was getting cold feet. In fact, the opposite was true. His friends expressed relief upon my return. They reported

Bob was wallowing in misery in my absence, haunted by the fear of losing me to some foreign lothario.

Our parents gave their blessings to a Thanksgiving wedding, which would be only for family and a few friends. Even though we were married in an ice storm that negated all extra festivities, we were eager to get started on our dream life together. Our parents were good examples for us, and our expectations were based on their lives.

Yet their model marriage was becoming obsolete in the sixties. America was on the verge of a major social and cultural upheaval that rejected traditional norms and values. Protest over the war in Vietnam was heating up, the big bands were losing out to the Beatles, and societal attitudes about sex and marriage were being overturned. Traditional roles, along with church and biblical values, were falling by the wayside. A cynical attitude about authority and institutions, especially church membership, and democratic ideals held sway.

These seismic shifts made our expectations impossible. The traditional role of homemakers was changing rapidly. Middle-class women were exchanging their housedresses and aprons for business attire, challenging the expectation that a woman's place was in the home by going off to work. This changing landscape created new conflicts, challenges, and expressions of anger and frustration with the status quo. A hit song by Nancy Sinatra—*These Boots Are Made for Walkin'*—reflected the feelings of many women struggling to find their place in what remained a male-dominated, double-standard society.

I had little awareness of the contradictions contained in this avalanche of change, or the cost of trying to resolve them. Nor did I suspect how rapidly traditional notions of marriage and family life were breaking down. For the first time in their lives, millions of women were asking the same question—*Who am I?*—when societal conventions collapsed.

At twenty-three, my idea of marriage was largely based on the example of my parents, who rarely engaged in open conflict. That lack of experience proved to be a liability when the inevitable disagreements with Bob, who lived in a more explosive family, occurred. Nor did I have an inkling of how much I didn't know about relationships or ingredients essential for a mature marriage. Getting married was simply the automatic next step after college—the path to the American dream of family and home most young, white, middle-class Americans took for granted as the socially and culturally "normal" thing to do.

What little I knew about Bob seemed more than enough. The qualities that impressed me most never wavered. People who knew and worked with Bob loved and adored him. He inspired loyalty and respect. That was the man whose character I witnessed throughout our six-month courtship. More importantly, he possessed the single-most, essential, top-of-the-list attribute required of my potential husband: he grew up Lutheran. Yet I knew almost nothing about his history and family or how they influenced his character.

During our courtship, I never doubted the sincerity of his beliefs or intentions, although it was never a topic of conversation. All the while we were dating, we attended church together, and

Bob was happy to have found a Christian to marry. My parents fell in love with Bob, especially my father, with whom he talked about God on his own, and they became close friends. So, no red flags there.

A few short months after the wedding, however, he hit me with a bombshell. As we were coming out of a Sunday service in which Dad's sermon focused on the meaning of the cross, Bob made a stunning confession: he couldn't believe the whole "cross thing"! Furthermore, he wasn't going to be a hypocrite by going to church without believing in the divinity of Jesus. This casual, matter-of-fact rejection of Christ stunned me. How did I miss such a fundamental fact? It never occurred to me that such a thing was possible—that someone could admire Christ's moral teachings yet deny His holiness. Having been fully immersed in a Christian worldview my whole life, I'd never known anyone who didn't believe this truth.

As it turned out, Bob admired the good character of Christian wives and was eager to marry someone who placed a high value on home and family. In the small-town Lutheran church where he grew up, it wasn't necessarily faith that drew people to worship but habit, family tradition, and community. Devoid of spiritual depth and meaning, Bob neither experienced nor believed in the mysterious, supernatural nature of the Trinity. Apart from the ethical values he heard lauded in church, faith was meaningless. I don't believe he purposefully hid this from me, or deliberately led me to think he was a Christian; he believed he *was* a Christian because he lived an ethical life. I mistakenly took his positive comments about the church at face value and simply assumed his outwardly expressed admiration reflected a deep inner conviction.

Bob's rejection of faith perfectly fit the temper of the times. A growing wave of skepticism long building in mainstream American life became a tidal wave in the mid-1960s. The culture was rejecting faith as a lie, a remnant of superstition leftover from a pre-science era. In the dawning age of cynicism and distrust of authority, Bob and many others saw atheism as the only intelligent alternative. For him, there was no resurrection, no life after death other than his legacy, which would live on through the solid character of his sons.

He never had a clue how deeply this gap affected me. Besides church being a cultured habit, his family's church attendance covered secrets about alcohol. Although he never complained about my involvement in church, there was a painful loneliness in sitting by myself as an organist and active Sunday school teacher. I rationalized and made up excuses for his absence, but inside I was deeply hurt. I held out hope that Bob would eventually change as he saw my faith in operation. Though we knew a deep love and cared about each other, sharing many wonderful times and common joys, our differences were a cause of distress for both of us.

I appreciated his honesty and refusal to live a lie, but the foundation of our marriage now held a crack. It was too painful to discuss, so we silently agreed to avoid the subject altogether. We were determined that our love would resolve our differences. In every other aspect, we were perfect for one another, holding the same values, goals, and dreams. I truly thought he would come to see the truth of the Christian life.

A born entrepreneur, Bob thrived on having many irons in the fire. Early in our marriage, he ran several businesses simultaneously, often working overtime to keep us financially afloat. He finally decided to focus on one of the business ventures, an income tax preparation service called TMI Inc., which required a heavy investment of time and money. To make sure his employees were well paid, we lived on borrowed money for several years. I taught sixth grade for a year and a half before my first pregnancy, but when I had to quit, our flow of income had to be supported by borrowed funds.

Until the late 1960s, H&R Block were the tax experts, and soon after Bob opened his first office, Tax Man Inc., Mr. Tax of America and other services joined the competition. Bob's genius for simplifying and organizing helped him create a tool called the TMI Tax Organizer. Clients could now bring their information all recorded in a three-page folder instead of in boxes. Twin City Federal invited TMI Inc. to office in their banks, and soon this untapped market helped establish Bob's business. His second and most successful venture was a product called the Tax Finder. Sold through conventions across the country, the Tax Finder became very popular among tax accountants who used it to complete their clients' tax forms more quickly and efficiently.

Bob's ingenuity made a real difference in people's lives. On learning that my husband created the book he was using, an IRS agent reviewing the tax forms of the nonprofit I worked for jumped over the desk to shake the hand of the wife of the man who made filing taxes easier. Not only did most income tax services purchase his book, but the Tax Finder was also a hit internationally. Eventually, TMI became a publisher.

In comparison to Bob's business, my life seemed dull and repetitive. But since family was a high priority for both of us, I needed to make some changes. Feeling frustrated and left behind, I decided to change my circumstances. First, I organized my day using my old teacher planner, which turned chaos into interesting days. My three little boys and I discovered lots of fun ways to spend those hours by using my teacher's skills. Then I decided to learn homemaking skills, sharpen my study plan, and establish a Bible study for the women in my neighborhood. That created deep relationships in our little community on the west end of Bush Lake. Last of all, I joined "The Generation Gap" made up of my old teacher friends who entertained with music and dance all over Minneapolis and St. Paul.

I also found ways to use my gifts and talents to help at my church, St. Michael's Lutheran in Bloomington. I missed interacting with young people. From my own checkered teenage years, I understood and empathized with the challenge of establishing one's own separate and unique identity, simultaneously respecting the boundaries set by parents and other adult authorities. I also knew the dangers of going off the rails. So, I became a Sunday school teacher of teens for a few years, which developed into a youth ministry called Joyful Noise. Those seven years were creative, stimulating, and highly successful in developing faith-filled teenagers. Joyful Noise is still going on today (forty-five years later) under the guidance of a youth pastor.

Our social life in Bloomington was never dull. We loved hosting parties, and our house quickly became the center of social life.

While alcohol always had a place on these occasions, it was never center stage, and Bob showed no signs or symptoms pointing to a problem. Many people drank socially without undue consequences. He blended well with our friends. I knew nothing about the cunning and insidious nature of alcoholism and its many disguises.

Over time, little clues started painting a darker picture. On returning home from a late-night rehearsal with The Generation Gap, I found Bob sound asleep at the top of the stairs, with two little boys crawling around the living room unsupervised, which, for him, was completely out of character. A burnt piece of toast or load of laundry left undone could upset him. Yet months often went by without incident; the storms were fleeting and unpredictable. For years, I talked myself into believing these increasingly brief and elusive periods of calm would last. When Bob did lose control, a hidden switch would flip, and he became someone I didn't recognize. It was frustrating, confusing, agonizing, and sometimes a little frightening. As black clouds gathered, I didn't dare raise the subject of his drinking and upset him.

By our seventh year of marriage, the problems became more difficult to deny. One truth I never suspected was my own part that kept the drama going. The word "codependent" describing me as the enabler in a dysfunctional relationship wasn't part of my vocabulary, nor could I see my reflection in that mirror. If I kept shoving my feelings under the rug, I enabled Bob to avoid facing the consequences of drinking. I vowed to do everything possible to keep our marriage and family intact.

Late one winter night in January 1975 toward the end of my pregnancy with Tyson, Bob stomped in the house after a long day at work and completely out of the blue announced, "I don't think I love you anymore. I want a divorce." He then careened back to the bedroom and collapsed on the bed in a stupor.

The dam inside me broke.

In a state of shock, I crouched down on the floor, bent over my belly filled with my third son, and wrapped in my own embrace, I shook with sobs of fear. Into this flood of feelings and confusion, the words of an unfamiliar Bible verse scrolled across my mind: "But whoso hearkeneth unto me shall dwell safely, and shall be quiet from fear of evil" (Proverbs 1:33, KJV). Huddled on the floor, the words began to sink in. I realized I had been given a way of safety, peace, and rest in the eye of the storm. The next morning, I looked up the unknown verse in my King James Bible. Proverbs 1:33 became the major change point for a radical new way of being in the world. From that day on, I vowed to hearken (hear and obey) every word of Scripture, to live as if God's promises were true. That same morning, Bob woke up as if nothing had happened.

A few days later, the long dormant nightmare of being buried alive returned. Once again, I was trapped in the mall dressing room, scurrying down the same narrowing tunnel, crawling toward the same fatal impasse. Yet the story had a different ending. When I reached the dead end this time, instead of panic, a flood of peace and calm flowed through me. I knew God was coming to my rescue. That nightmare never haunted me again.

Though Bob and I never discussed what happened that night, I devoted myself to study, determined to live by the book, which increased my joy and love for my husband and family life.

Yet more troubles lay ahead.

As was my habit after each meeting of Joyful Noise, I met my coleader at a restaurant to debrief the evening. We sat in a quiet booth with soothing elevator music unobtrusively playing in the background. A door suddenly opened, and billows of cigarette smoke belched out—along with the intrusive noise of a cranked-up jukebox, jolting our conversation. Throughout that evening we would be stopped mid-sentence and wait silently for the door to swing shut. Warily, we'd pick up the conversation, knowing it could swing open at any moment and put us back in limbo. It was a perfect metaphor for my life back then—stretches of smooth sailing when Bob was at his best, interrupted by squalls and dark clouds.

Not only was Bob a committed skeptic, but our large group of brilliant and accomplished friends shared his unbelief. Because our closest friends came out of *his* life, and the couples were, like Bob, uninvolved with any church, I once again was a minority of one—often having to defend my beliefs. They often barraged me with questions I couldn't answer. The relentless badgering left me feeling beat up, misunderstood, and alone. I dove deeper into Scripture. Thus began the many hours of discovery that the Bible was authentic, historical, and reliable beyond all other ancient texts. The more knowledge and understanding I gained, the more skilled I became at responding to my skeptical friends. Once I could answer their questions, the attacks mysteriously subsided and eventually stopped. That's when it dawned on me. They were never interested in the subject of faith; they either just loved the debate or were unable to argue with the truth.

In the struggle for balance, I wrote my father for advice. "I feel confident that the Bible gives priority to the family in the service of the Lord," he wrote back. "Don't put church in competition with your family responsibilities, especially while your children are young and need your loving attention and guidance. The church, like the poor, will always be there to serve, but your children are rapidly growing up." Today, I count those years priceless and am grateful I was there to influence their lives.

On the afternoon of May 1977, I was driving through Bloomington on my way home from a meeting with Joyful Noise leaders, when I heard the Lord say, "It is time to resign your position." Confused by this startling news, I pulled off the road.

"Really?" I said with disappointment in my voice. "It's going so strong. Why now?" But the message was loud and clear—and I knew it wasn't my idea. God had spoken. Within the next month, Bob started talking about wanting to move to a small town. Imagine his surprise at discovering I'd already resigned and was ready for a new life.

After searching for towns within a sixty-mile radius of the Twin Cities, we found a 1950s rambler on Lake Waconia. Bob was excited about it, but to me, it looked dark and dreary and in need of work. We had just finished remodeling our house in Bloomington, and I didn't want to live in sawdust anymore.

On the way home, Bob handed me a check, saying, "I believe this is the house." I was not so sure. He asked me to give it one more look, and if I approved, I was to give the realtor a check for the down payment. "If not," he said, "we'll find another."

Though my mind was made up against it, I agreed to give 227 Lakeview Terrace one more look. As I pulled into the driveway and parked, I saw the strangest thing. The drab exterior was now bathed in a golden light. I skipped the walk-through and with a steady hand signed the check and gave it to the realtor, confident of God's sign.

REFLECTION

God is always up to something, and He takes your life more seriously than you do. Can you say, "Good!" when a door closes instead of opens? That can only happen when you accept the reality that God is training you for a larger life than you can fathom. His training includes setbacks, challenges, failures, and rejections to strengthen your inner spirit, not defeat it. The key is to read the Word as your personal guide in a confusing culture of values, pressures to perform, and self-centered attitudes.

Christians are given a different perspective, resource center, purpose for their lives, and empowerment when they are born again into the realm of heaven. Being a Christian is not a belief system...it is a life system.

DISCUSSION

It is important to know that God-life (*zoe*, the life force of God) has been installed in your spirit and is activated to train, empower, guide, protect, and inspire you for an eternal life now. To walk the earth as Jesus walked is possible because you have the Holy Spirit-inspired Word in your hands.

1. How real is being born again for you?

2. What does this have to do with the concept of a blessing house?

ACTION

I challenge you to read the Scriptures, not just to answer questions, but to think of the Word as the singular resource for life as Jesus lived. Instead of translating it to your lifestyle, let it translate your human life into life in the Spirit. That will mean learning what the words mean.

Perhaps it is time to get a Bible dictionary that includes Greek and Hebrew meanings. It will increase your wisdom and love of God's Word. For example, studying that being *jealous* of another means you wish you had what the other person has. The word *covet* goes deeper. It means you wish you had it and the other person didn't have it. This study of the Word helped me understand how deep sin goes so I could repent and repair a relationship.

CHAPTER SEVEN

THE DOORKEEPER

"Better is one day in your courts than a thousand elsewhere. I would rather be a doorkeeper in the house of the Lord, than dwell in the tents of the wicked."
(PSALM 84:10, NIV)

Kyle, Ryan, and Tyson were eight, seven, and three when we moved to Waconia, a small town of about 2,500 in 1978. Bob thought the relative peace and tranquility with a slower pace of life would be good for our family and reduce his stress, making it easier to stop drinking. Years later I learned that believing a change in environment alone is enough to help control drinking habits is common alcoholic thinking. While it may be an essential step in the process of recovery, it is only one of the many steps required to achieve sobriety.

Like Bob, I also wanted to believe the answer to our problems could be so simple, but I wondered about the impact of the change on me and the boys. Bob deserved the benefit of the doubt, and this move would settle the issues. At the time, I didn't know the cunning, baffling, and powerful nature of alcoholism, nor the profound changes of deeply rooted feeling, thought, and behavior needed to deal with the disease, including my own codependent thinking.

We were excited to start a new life and moved that June so the boys could join summer programs and find friends quickly. We crossed paths with our friends and neighbors at church, the golf club, school, and shopping. Living on a lake was a whole new reality of a community who loved the water, boats, fishing, and swimming. Looking out the windows each morning as the sun changed the colors of the sky, I got a glimpse of the sublime.

On Lake Waconia, our family quickly became part of the sports and recreation crowd at the golf course, school events, and, of course, the lake. We truly enjoyed our community and became leaders in several organizations. Bob taught the boys building skills as they helped change the landscape and lakeshore into a wonderland for our friends and families. They took full advantage of the lake, woods, and open fields to go hunting and three-wheeling.

The biggest culture shock came from switching churches, from the more orthodox St. Michael's Lutheran in Bloomington to the more liberal Faith Lutheran (Evangelical Lutheran Church of America) in Waconia. I didn't know much about Faith Lutheran but had heard good things about its commitment to nurturing social and community connection. Having been active in my other churches, I looked forward to getting involved. In a few short months, however, I found myself at odds with the pastor's theology. One Saturday I came face-to-face with the angry founding pastor, who took an opposite view of Scripture.

"You will destroy this church if you stay," he railed at me. "Others believe like you do, but they don't talk like you do," he shouted.

"I can't leave because my husband chose this church."

"Well, keep quiet and just pour coffee," he ordered.

Bob, incensed by the pastor's reaction, said, "Well, if he can't recognize a real Christian when he sees one, I'm not going back."

Bob left immediately, the pastor took another call within a few months, but the boys and I stayed twenty-five years. I became the Christian education director, instructed Bible classes, and promoted new programs with the next three pastors. Years later, a member of the congregation told me, "You were just what this church needed."

"Why would you say that?"

"Because you're a woman of conviction," he replied.

When my father died of a massive heart attack at the age of sixty-seven, we moved Mother to an apartment in Waconia, and I dedicated the year to getting her acclimated to her new surroundings. The next summer, doctors discovered a grapefruit-sized tumor in her brain that had been growing silently for years and gave her three months to live. She moved in with us. There was a lot of turmoil in our already busy house at the time when Mother needed extensive attention. Though her doctors had given her three months, she lived three more years during which her steadily declining physical health and onset of dementia required constant, increasing attention. I had just been elected to the Waconia School Board, Bob's drinking was escalating, and Tyson, age eleven, was now experimenting with drugs and alcohol.

Except for my high-achieving sons, Kyle and Ryan, I felt like the only other sane one in the house. Yet my hold was slipping. One cold and blustery October afternoon, I reached my limit. The cauldron of pain and disappointment inside boiled over. Distraught and defeated by a list of overwhelming demands and responsibilities, I couldn't stay in the madhouse a minute longer or risk becoming unglued myself. I grabbed my jacket and walked out the door.

It was bitter cold walking four blocks without a destination. I found myself standing at the doors of our church, which happened to be open. I walked in and collapsed into a pew at the back of the sanctuary. The next few hours were spent in tears and prayer.

Please don't make me go back. I can't do this anymore. Don't make me. Don't ask me to go back.

I wept until I was dry eyed asking God to free me from the pressure I was under.

Let me stay here and serve You here. I will be the doorkeeper in the house of the Lord and serve You as if it were my home. I promised to open the doors and greet the people, fix and pour coffee between services, clean the church—anything.

Just don't tell me to go back.

No word, no verse, no sound, only a deep, empty silence. I was suspended in time for several hours, helpless and hopeless.

I'd come to be rescued, but I felt even more abandoned and alone. The afternoon had drifted into a dark and gloomy evening by the time I trudged home through the sleet and wind, exhausted and dejected. My hopes and prayers to be released from the exhausting burden of caring for three people who couldn't be helped went unanswered, so I resigned myself to reentering a home where I felt defeated and crushed by the weight of everyone else's needs and expectations. I reached the front door with trepidation.

At that very moment, standing at the threshold with my hand ready to turn the knob, I clearly heard a voice say, *"This is the house of the Lord, and you are the doorkeeper."* There was nothing cryptic about the message; I knew exactly what it meant. Though it wasn't the answer I expected, I felt an immediate strength and renewal of hope pour into me. It was God's reassurance that I was in the right place, at the right time, doing the right thing. I left home that afternoon feeling trapped by circumstances. I returned to a deeper truth; it wasn't me who was trapped. This truly was my assignment. I was the doorkeeper of this house in this town. From that day on, I was no longer a victim but empowered by God's authority to shape my surroundings and to stand guard over the spiritual and physical well-being of my family.

Amidst all the chaos and confusion, I'd forgotten the simple, yet essential, foundation of my existence. My name is Gail, "a father's joy"—"You love righteousness and hate wickedness; therefore God, your God, has set you above your companions by anointing you with the oil of joy" (Psalm 45:7, NIV). But what did it mean to *be a source of joy* in a house that felt anything but joyful? What exactly did it mean in practical terms? To fulfill my purpose, I needed to delve more deeply into the practical ways of manifesting joy.

For many people, this word conjures images of exuberant happiness—a good feeling that shouts, "I love you!" from a rooftop, jumps up and down with glee, dances, and buys a round of drinks to mark the occasion. But this is not what joy means in Scripture. In his autobiography, *Surprised by Joy*, author C. S. Lewis distinguishes capital "J" Joy from its lower-case cousin by its *source*. Lewis experienced an unexplained joy three different times: first as a young boy with a toy garden in the nursery, then a sense of desire of incalculable worth as from another dimension, and finally as an experience of being uplifted to regions in the northern sky. "Anyone who has experienced it will want it again. All joy reminds you that it is never a possession, but desire for something long ago or further away or still to be."[6] This joy was the pointer to Jesus Christ as the Son of God.

If I am a Father's Joy, I am a *source* of Joy because I have a supernatural wellspring that never runs dry. It's a kind of Joy that can't be manufactured from matter, but only inspired and continually regenerated from Scripture. Joy would later become the most essential ingredient, indeed the very foundation of the Blessing House.

"This is the house of the Lord, and you are the doorkeeper." Those life-changing words shed new light on my situation. God's reassurance that I was in the *right place*, at the *right time*, doing the *right thing*, quelled my anxious soul. The present turmoil was

---

6 C. S. Lewis, *Surprised by Joy: The Shape of My Early Life* (San Diego, CA: Harcourt, Brace & World, 1956), 10–11.

but a fleeting moment in a chapter of my story, leading not to defeat but victory.

Well, all right, I thought. *Now I know the way. I know* this *is where I'm supposed to be.* This *is my assignment. I am to be the doorkeeper of* this *house. I'm the wife of* this *husband, the mother of* these *boys, the daughter of* this *mother. However difficult, God will give me all the wisdom I need to complete it.*

Running away wouldn't cure my affliction. God had already given me the peace my soul so desperately sought. The fount of everlasting life already overflowed within me. The message received in Waconia that October afternoon confirmed that, despite my frustrations and feelings of going nowhere, I was in exactly the right place at the right time. Our home at Lakeview Terrace was a "thin place" where the worlds of matter and spirit merged.

Knowing at a deep level this home was, indeed, where God wanted me to be and I wasn't struggling in vain was another crucial change point in my life. As my anxiety and despair lifted and the path before me cleared, confidence in the alignment of my soul with the calling of the Holy Spirit grew stronger. While my material circumstances remained the same, Scripture radically shifted my focus from the material to the spiritual world. This, in turn, not only lifted my discouraged heart but gave me the perspective to appreciate and learn from my present situation. A clearer understanding of my role in our family gave me the spiritual insight and authority needed to be the doorkeeper, to stand guard over the moral and spiritual influences flowing in and out of our home.

The balance of power in our marriage also shifted for the better as the division of authority between Bob and me became more distinct. He exercised authority in the material realm, while I took charge in the spiritual. My power in the spiritual realm was profoundly the meaning of my name. It became real to me that Bob was trapped in an alcoholic daze...and I was not. The enemy was using Bob's tongue to defeat me. I realized I had the life force of God to love the one who could not love me back.

REFLECTION

We all experience times in our lives when we feel trapped by circumstance. We may feel imprisoned by the past—traumatic or abusive childhood experiences, for example—afraid of future disaster, or bound by destructive habits to numb physical, emotional, mental, or spiritual suffering. It may be difficult to escape the despair that often accompanies feeling trapped—the feeling of hopelessness that no matter what we do, how hard we try, how devoutly we pray, our fate is sealed. Yet we needn't sleepwalk through life, busily distracting ourselves from living.

What would it be like to live within that same space absorbing the beauty and sound and sight in the present moment? One would need a four-dimensional existence or maybe more to see into the deeper realities of what we are all about. We say goodbye at the door and walk away rather than lingering over another's footsteps as they leave us behind. We pass one another in our journeys hardly having time to really see and experience all we are to each other. How did we change one another? How did we affect our futures or enrich our pasts?

I wonder if heaven will be that wonderland of multilayered life within each passing, where there is no time sequence. Will we be able to take in the red tablecloth, the shadows and layered view through the blinds to the patio tables? Will we hear the music of the tree limbs as the wind passes through, even as our eyes chase a leaf across the stone floor? What about the contrast of colors on the marbled oak church bench as the sunlight plays its dance and the rag rugs woven from multicolored wool strips that adorn its seat? Will we be able to take all that in even as we sit at coffee with an old friend weaving a morning tale? Will we be able to live fully each moment? Is there a moment in a "no time" zone? God is always a NOW God. Is my desire to be alive to all I see and hear a reflection of yearning for His presence?

DISCUSSION

1. This world is not your real home, for you belong to a greater kingdom that operates on different values, sense of purpose, and destiny.

2. What is the value of seeing life from God's perspective instead of your own?

3. What does it feel like to be in this world system and yet not of it?

ACTION

It is important to build a library to enrich and expand your understanding of who you are as a citizen of heaven living in this time and space in this neighborhood with these family members and understanding your mission from the Lord. (See the recommended reading list at the end of this book for works that were instrumental in teaching me about this extraordinary life.)

1. I suggest reading the book *Walking in This World: The Practical Art of Creativity* by Julia Cameron to help you get in touch with yourself, your interests, gifts, experiences, and surprise realities that will open your life to yourself. Cameron challenges you with three basic tools: "morning pages, artist date, and a weekly walk."[7] Not to miss!

2. Take a class on helping you discover your spiritual gifts. It will bring clarity on how God could use your talents or gifts.

3. Consider investing in a life coach. It's very rewarding to have someone to help you with a life review. I personally benefited from exploring my life, my background, my giftings, patterns of behavior that created roadblocks in my life, and misbeliefs that kept me from achieving my goals.

---

7 Julia Cameron, *Walking in This World: The Practical Art of Creativity* (New York: Jeremy P. Tarcher/Penguin, 2002).

CHAPTER EIGHT

GOD'S GIFTS COME IN STRANGE PACKAGES

"God often uses those we least expect to accomplish His greatest works."[8]

KURT BRUNER AND JIM WARE,
FINDING GOD IN THE LORD OF THE RINGS

Bob was a highly successful businessman, a pillar of the community, and a dedicated family man who did not manifest the symptoms of financial distress that typically accompanies alcoholism. Friends and relatives covered for him, built a wall of secrecy behind which he could hide. But their misguided loyalty slowly destroyed the person they tried to protect.

---

8 Kurt Bruner and Jim Ware, *Finding God in the Lord of the Rings* (Wheaton, Ill: Tyndale House. 2001).

He was trapped both by the disease and the things in his past neither of us knew or understood, plus a generational straitjacket of addiction from which he could not free himself. Growing up, he took on the role of hero, rescuer, and provider. Young and old wanted Bob to weigh in before making any major financial decisions. His whole identity rested on being the strong, successful one in the family, the godfather whom everyone looked up to and sought out for advice. More poisonous than alcohol was the stubborn, foolish, deadly pride to which all of us are prone. To the bitter end, he was more concerned about hiding his shame than making peace with himself.

"Don't go blabbing this around," he instructed me at the hospital in Waconia. "They don't even know what's wrong with me." This was just after the surrounding doctors said he had lost pints of blood and was in dangerous trouble from esophageal bleeding.

Watching my husband of twenty-eight years self-destruct by degrees and being helpless to stop it was painful. At times it was a grueling ordeal that tested the limits of my faith. The confusion of all going well, then the sudden slide into unexplained hostility left me very lonely. Yet, I knew that if I never married again, I would have known a deep and passionate love. The last years together I just never knew which Bob was going to show up and what new lessons were coming toward me.

His skeptical, even cynical, attitude toward the church forced me to confront the paradoxes, contradictions, and complications in my own life of faith. He never let me off the hook or slide by on slogans, pious phrases, pretenses, or rituals. Though he did not defeat his demons, Bob taught me things about love and faith I could not have learned any other way. Had he not pushed all my buttons, had I not needed to place all my trust in God alone, I never would have known the truth and power of God in real life situations.

His cardinal virtues were honesty and humility. With him, what you saw was what you got. He couldn't tolerate fakes or phonies and could spot hypocrisy a mile away. If people didn't act consistently with their beliefs, he said, they were all a charade. It was ironic that he died because he couldn't face that in himself.

Bob became both my greatest critic and the strengthener of my faith. He challenged me more than anyone I've known to live the truths I claimed to believe. Without his constant testing and questioning, I might have played at being a Christian but missed the true meaning of my lines. It would have all been a performance, convincing to many, perhaps, but still only a facsimile of faith, not the thing itself.

Having grown up immersed in the culture of Christianity and drawing on my pedigree, I could talk the talk as well as anyone. Living with Bob, however, gave me nowhere to hide. He presented me with a stark choice to be the real deal or play let's pretend. There was no in-between. Etched on his gravestone is the meaning of his name, "Man of Excellent Worth," and Psalm 15 describes his character. This is the priceless legacy he left us.

I fell in love with the heart of Bob Berger because it was open, available, kind, and generous with himself and people from all walks of life. His legacy to his sons is his heart, because all three of them reflect this same nature.

Bob's instincts about the benefits of a small-town life initially panned out. The move to Waconia fulfilled its promise, even though, like many small towns, it was culturally a drinking society. We loved the summer months when he could be home because the long, winter tax seasons required exhausting days. During those months, the best plan was for Bob to stay every other night in his Hopkin's office instead of driving the long way home. That was when signs and symptoms, such as glazed eyes, slurred speech, and mood swings, became noticeable. His perception of the family ranged from being "the greatest" to "the worst" in a flash. Ten years after moving to Waconia, I saw all the same problems that had surfaced in Bloomington, Minnesota.

I did my best to shield our boys from these issues. Things improved immensely when we attended a weekend marriage encounter, but in the end, going to Al Anon was the smartest thing I did. I thought the doctor's warning to Bob about the alcohol issue would have reinforced the positive things that were happening. But his steady descent into denial could only be stopped with an intervention, which proved to be a complex process with attorneys, courts, the bank, law enforcement, witnesses, and cooperation of our boys who were in junior high school.

"Either go into treatment or we need to separate" was the ultimatum. I watched his heart contract and grow cold, but he was willing to cooperate. He was told by his treatment counselor that if he didn't stop drinking, he would be dead in ten years. His sobriety lasted for four years until he decided to "take back his life." He died ten years from the intervention.

There is an old proverb that says, "A man takes a drink. A drink takes a drink. The drink takes the man." Six years later the warning came true.

Bob couldn't bear the pain of accepting that he needed help, much less let others see his vulnerability. For him, giving up the role of family hero was equivalent to death. Despite all the good he'd done, all the hardships overcome, he still felt the need for a drink to quiet the fears. That was the great tragedy—there was nothing to prove. He already was a hero in our eyes. By accepting his vulnerability, he would not have fallen from grace but gained more.

He simply didn't know how to recreate a life for himself without alcohol. His intelligence and financial success, which he used as a defense, sadly worked against him. He was too proud to admit or accept the help he needed to heal. The well of shame inside him must have felt bottomless. It was agonizing to watch this talented, loving husband and father slowly drink himself to death.

The result was a tragic, watershed moment in his life and our marriage. Though he grudgingly went through the motions of his treatment program, he never forgave what he considered my "stab in the back," never spoke to the friends of thirty years who participated in the intervention, and never worked through his shame and humiliation. In bringing his addiction to light, he felt I had wiped out everything he held dear: his self-esteem, reputation, and friendships.

The two eldest boys were now graduated from college with great futures ahead, and the youngest was soon to graduate from high school when Bob's body gave out the week of Memorial Day, 1993. Bob experienced esophageal bleeding, meaning that his blood could no longer get through the liver and exploded into his digestive system. He collapsed on the couch.

"I'm calling the ambulance!"

"You don't need to do that!" he ordered. Casting about for someone to help, I saw a doctor friend of mine right outside my window.

"What are you doing here?" I hollered.

"Looking for rose trellises. I thought you would have some in your gardens."

"No...you are here to help me get Bob to the hospital!" One look at Bob and he ordered the ambulance.

While we waited, Bob took my hand as he lay on the couch and said, "I want you to know how much it meant that you never said no to me." I never knew that he recognized the difficulties of staying loving with my servant spirit.

The hospital removed five pints of bile from his extended belly, gave him the needed transfusions, and arranged for him to be transferred downtown. With that settled, I called the boys and told them what happened and fell asleep on the couch in his hospital room.

The next morning, I found him in a straitjacket and sedated to keep him quiet and from tearing out the tubes. He had gone into delirium tremens and saw snakes and demons on the ceiling. Inside, I was frozen into stillness with the reality that he wasn't going to make it. Tyson was home, and Kyle and Ryan arrived in the next twenty-four hours from Cleveland and California. Bob was hooked up to the machines and could only respond by squeezing a finger to say yes or no to questions. The doctor came in to ask about turning off the machines. I was unable to answer and grateful that Ryan said, "No. Not until Kyle arrives and sees Dad."

The hours crawled by, and each of the three boys was able to spend time alone with him to say what they needed in their love and forgiveness. Bob died peacefully with all of us around him saying the Lord's prayer and the twenty-third Psalm. The battle was over.

The night before, a nurse on the night shift asked me about our family. She said they almost never saw a loving family attend such a death because of the destruction in relationships. I was able to speak to her about the power and love available for a life through Christ. As we left arm in arm, Kyle said, "We have done all things well, Mom."

The next days were a blur dealing with the community of friends, family, and neighbors celebrating his life and influence. That same week, my youngest son graduated from high school, and the world around us was spinning. After the exhausting days, I had time to ask my neighbor (the doctor in the window) why he appeared when he did.

"I was reading the Sunday paper and saw rose bushes for sale, and I began wondering if you had any rose trellises. I wanted to see what you had before I went to the store." Stunned, his wife had decided to join him as they walked several blocks to my window because he had never ever been interested in gardening, let alone roses.

Because of Bob's last words to me and the timely appearance of a doctor looking for roses, I knew that the Lord had tended to Bob's death and received him into His kingdom. He was like the thief on the cross who came within moments of his death to receive the gospel of love through our covering of loving words and prayers. A man lost in addictions can still be found by the Savior even to the last moments.

SPIDERMAN

Fragile is the web of lies
A man secures himself in.
He spins a pattern with his words
Woven from his store of times
to complete a web unique.
Lit in the sun by sparkled rain
It seems a thing of beauty
Surrounded in his woven words
He waits to catch, to feed
And grow on others
caught within.
Vulnerable to all of life
Yet proud and boastful of his work
To prove himself a worthy man,
He spins by natural means
A labyrinth of excuse and reasons
Why he isn't free to fly and soar
And move unbounded.
His web turns dusty
Gets heavy with dirt
And yet He clings
To fragile things
To give his life a meaning.

—GAIL BERGER

REFLECTION

Retracing your life experiences from God's perspective and the Word of God allows freedom to explore what has been accomplished through both good and bad times. No one gets through life without challenges, so it is important to understand the ways of God and the inestimable value of living by the truths of Scripture. One must learn to say no to their own reactions, perspectives, and decisions when they contradict God's principles and laws. My life and my family's life were secured despite the destructive force of alcoholism because I learned to hear, trust, and obey daily. I also learned to take advantage of all the resources available without shame or guilt.

Whenever I was feeling beat up, discouraged, angry, and worthless, I learned to set the alarm for fifteen to thirty minutes to truly express and feel deeply what I was going through. When the ringer sounded, it was time to go back to work on a goal or project.

Giving myself space to acknowledge and feel the rawness gave me control over my emotions instead of ignoring them. They needed to be voiced so they no longer had the upper hand. I learned to do a lot of things, create new projects, and train myself in physical exercise. When Bob died, it was difficult to readjust and solve new problems...but I was prepared by my past experiences.

DISCUSSION

Life and death need to be thought out. Remembering and dreaming, making lists, and keeping journals, asking good questions, and self-educating are always up to you. No one can do it for you. Staying trapped in your circumstances is not an option for a Christian who has the life of God flowing in their spirit.

God can use anyone or anything for His glory. According to First Corinthians 1:26–29, He chooses the things the world dismisses. He shows Himself strong with the weak; He shows himself generous with the poor; He shows himself loving with the meek. Do not negate what you have experienced and learned because those very things can make you valuable to others. Don't think you have to be perfect and have it all together to bring value to the kingdom.

As you are establishing your path to hospitality, you will need to learn to practice one of God's greatest gifts, which is refusing to pick up an offense. I have learned that the enemy's favorite weapons against you is destroying relationships and futures by using someone's mouth to offend us. Refuse that temptation and exercise the power to walk away free and make the enemy miserable. Be at peace and open potential gifts for your future.

ACTION

If you feel trapped, make a firm decision to move forward by evaluating these questions:

1. What lies are you listening to?

2. In what ways have you changed in the last year?

3. What are you learning through classes, support groups, teachings?

4. What kind of relationship have you formed with the Lord Himself?

5. How lazy are you, fearful and anxious, or trapped in self-pity?

Set the timer to sit and feel what you feel. Get to know the truths of the God-life within you...and learn to worship your Creator and Savior in a personal way.

PART II

SPACES FOR GOD TO WORK

CHAPTER NINE

ROOMS OF MY OWN

"If one advances confidently in the direction of his dreams,
and endeavors to live the life which he has imagined,
he will meet with a success unexpected in common hours."[9]
—HENRY DAVID THOREAU

At age fifty, I finally had a bedroom of my own, a whole houseful of rooms in fact, and plenty of time and space to dream. The resources inherited from Bob now gave me the financial freedom to create a future unfettered by fear. But the transition from wife to widowhood wasn't easy. The empty chair at the dinner table, his former command post, was a constant reminder of his absence and the life I left behind. His death left a gaping hole, and as a wife and mother, I followed him into the grave.

---

9 Thoreau, *Walden*.

It took a long time and the shedding of many tears to claw myself out of the hole of grief and loss. Despite our difficulties, I deeply loved the man, appreciated his strengths, and empathized with his weaknesses. Overall, our marriage was a happy one. With the addition of three boys, our life in Bloomington was idyllic. The boys thrived in a home surrounded by forested land with a pond and sledding hill that begged for exploration and adventure. Our years in Waconia were also filled with family, fun, laughter, and friends.

As a world of new possibilities opened, many of the habits and routines that structured my life—even the names and days of the week—could be changed. *Today should be a Monday,* I wrote in my journal, *but it's New Life Day in my world.* Over time, I began thinking of the days of the week differently—Monday became New Life Day; Tuesday, Bible Study Day, Wednesday, Golf Day; and so on, based on classes or activities. If I could rename the days of the week, what else was possible?

I found myself in the enviable position of being able to create my life anew, with no strict rules or regulations or fear of money problems hanging over my head. I was free to control my comings and goings, to wake up and go to bed when I wanted, to switch at will my perspective on the meaning and purpose of night and day. But what purpose should all that freedom serve? I had to confront the mystery of what life meant to me—and how I'd choose to live it.

Money certainly didn't solve the mystery or make that question any easier. Although Bob and I had money to live well, we never wanted to stand out. We were delighted to live an average lifestyle well within our means. The desire to have more stuff was never a temptation for us. With more than my day-to-day needs met, I could choose to live however and wherever I wanted. I could go in any direction, but where was God calling me to go?

Calculating my value based on what I could accomplish, rather than my value to God, could lead me astray. Time had to slow down for me to hear and let God's voice guide me amidst all the possible options. "Wait on the Lord," the psalmist wrote, "be of good courage, and he shall strengthen thine heart: wait, I say, on the Lord" (Psalm 27:14, KJV). I don't like to play the waiting game. I always loved action and adventure. Yet, as Virginia Woolf wrote in "A Room of One's Own," "It is in our idleness, in our dreams, that submerged truth sometimes comes to the top."[10]

Before making any major life changes, I first had to get a grip on my finances—an area in which my experience was limited to say the least. Bob had always managed the budget, giving me money for household expenses, which I reported monthly. We jokingly called it my "fudget" because I kept such poor records. Now that I owned all our assets, I needed a team of trustworthy advisors to help me make good decisions. Even with my team, I was plunged into an alien world of confusing facts and figures, in charge of managing large sums without the most rudimentary knowledge, experience, and skills. Financial managers spoke a

10 Virginia Woolf, "A Room of One's Own" (England: Hogarth Press, 1929).

strange language peppered with an arcane vocabulary that, even translated into layman's terms, was hard to digest.

One of the first priorities was choosing Bob's replacement in his business. Our eldest son, Kyle, whose business and leadership skills had already been recognized by Harvey McKay, best-selling author of *How to Swim with the Sharks Without Getting Eaten Alive*, was the obvious choice. In developing and marketing a series of highly successful business leadership conferences, McKay had personally recruited a small group of young men, including Kyle, who modeled the confidence and executive skills developed in his conferences as his personal representatives to corporate clients nationwide. In that role, Kyle had the rare opportunity to work closely with a world-class business leader. Ryan, Tyson, and I were invited to attend these conferences, which we all did together and learned valuable leadership skills we could apply in our own lives.

In the meantime, dealing with lawyers and CPAs, reorganization plans, and forming a new board of directors were just a few of the challenges before me. My financial advisors were graceful, knowledgeable men, but accustomed to building wealth, not giving it away, as their top priority. They lacked the experience to advise a woman for whom philanthropy came first. I had the funds but no guidelines, goals, or criteria by which to evaluate requests from worthy causes. I later learned that many widows find themselves in the same boat, vulnerable to friends who need money.

I was invited to join Royal Treasure, a national association that helped wealthy women learn how to handle money, especially how to *give it away* wisely. My first act was to give each of my sons $10,000 (an allowed, tax-free gift) with the caveat that they spend $3,000 on a nice vacation and give away $7,000 to charity. My goal was for them to experience the joy of generosity. To this day, they continue to practice generous giving.

As financial matters fell into place and I began envisioning my future, the question came: What was God calling me to do with the abundance given me? Though I had financial freedom and the space to express my creativity, what was He calling me to create? I asked myself, "Now, how can I bless my world?"

Why not bless my world by sharing my house on Lakeview Terrace with others? If Moses could use his staff to beat the heck out of Pharaoh, what could I do with a house on a lake!

I began looking at everything with a new eye. How might I redesign the space to make every inch a place for God to work in people's lives? Drawing on my own experience, I imagined how the spaces would stimulate rich and enlivening interactions among guests. But how to translate such a vision into material reality was a challenge. What would make the space feel warm and welcoming, a place of peace, prayer, and community? How might the current layout be reconfigured? How might the walls, floors, and ceilings of such a house look, a house where every square inch evoked a sense of wonder, enchantment, and mystery? What kinds of features, qualities, characteristics, and arrangements of the objects in the rooms, and the flow between them, would be most conducive to manifesting the beautiful, yet unseen realm of spirit?

As these thoughts continued percolating, I began working toward another goal to which my heart had long been led. In January 1994, I enrolled in a master of divinity degree program at

Luther Theological Seminary in St. Paul. Years earlier, I'd heeded my father's wise advice to put service to my family first. Yet I was now in a new phase of life as a single woman. My life had a focus, a direction, a way forward.

I knew I wanted to serve God with all my heart, mind, and soul and needed the credibility of the degree to open a broader range of options. I didn't want to squeeze my calling into a conventional role as missionary, pastor, chaplain, or director of Christian education. Instead, I felt drawn to use my faith experiences, knowledge, gifts, and resources to bless my world from the place I heard God's voice the loudest: my home.

Unbeknownst to me, however, God was brewing a bigger story as I shuttled back and forth from my house in Waconia to the seminary. He not only handed me a more variegated palette with which to start painting my future, He expanded the size of my canvas by inserting an unexpected love story into my life.

"Hey, Gail, this is Jerry. I was wondering if you'd like to have dinner with me Friday night?"

I knew the voice on the other end of the line but was caught off guard by his question. Jerry Stangret was a friend and neighbor from Waconia who belonged to the same golf club. I knew Jerry as a nice guy divorced with four grown sons with whom he had great relationships. I knew that he played with his grandchildren and had reconciled with his ex-wife. He was also a successful business owner, a developer, and builder of elevators. I'd never thought of him as someone I would date.

Hmm. Would I like that? I wasn't so sure. Was he asking for a date?

"What if I picked you up Friday night and we enjoyed an early Italian dinner together?"

Oh, dear, I thought. *Now what?* I'd just begun my first year at seminary and had no desire to complicate my plans by adding a romantic relationship. He was also a lapsed Catholic who didn't attend church, and here I was deeply involved in and committing to become a Lutheran pastor! He only had a high school education, and I was pursuing a master's and eventually a doctoral degree in divinity. When and how our marriages ended were also both so different. He and his wife had been divorced for nine years, while I was recently widowed. My initial instinct was to politely decline as the voice inside urged me.

I paused to reflect. On the other hand, what would it hurt to say yes? What was wrong with an early Italian dinner with a nice man? So, I nervously accepted his invitation. Hanging up, I remember wondering, *What the heck does one do on a date?* I hadn't gone out with anyone since my dates with Bob more than thirty years ago.

Jerry picked me up in a big black truck and had to help me climb, awkwardly, into my seat. On the way to the restaurant, we talked about our sons and golf, mercifully arriving before the shallow well of small talk went dry. It was all uphill from there—a long night of struggling to stay awake while listening to an interminable monologue detailing the rise and fall of his marriage and divorce. Not exactly my idea of a good time!

This being my first date in a very long time, I wondered about the protocol as he drove me home and we pulled into the driveway. From Jerry's general demeanor, I could tell he was equally adrift. He kept his seatbelt fastened tight as I said goodbye, and I slid out the door. The garage door took forever opening as I awkwardly waited exposed in his headlights.

Thank goodness that's over! I thought as he drove off. *I'm never doing that again! That stupid date was as bad as it could be. What was I thinking?* Two weeks later, the phone rang again.

"I have two tickets for the piano concert over at Northrup Auditorium, center section, eight rows back," Jerry said.

Once again, my feelings were mixed. My plans to decline were thwarted by the headline performer, George Winston, my favorite pianist, whom I never expected to see play in concert. Here was a mystery. Jerry didn't seem culturally inclined, so how on earth could he have known his invitation would be irresistible? Even so, why go to all the trouble of finding out after our first—and what I hoped would be our last—date was such a disaster? I was intrigued. *This guy is cleverer than he lets on.* So, I bit my lip and said, "Yes, I'd love to go."

In the following weeks, I saw Jerry change before my very eyes—or rather my perception of him altered. When I stopped viewing him through the shallow lens of external attributes, something miraculous happened. As the scales fell from my eyes, I began to see my own blindness. As always, God had a better plot in mind. When my preconceptions of him fell away, a wonderful human being emerged: a person of interest, a good friend, and a potential life partner. Jerry didn't need to change for this love story to begin. I did.

Jerry had many of the same good qualities I admired in Bob—a total lack of pretense; a hearty, honest personality that was easy and fun to be around; and high moral standards—but there were also some surprises. Not only did I learn to keep my distance whenever he swung a golf club, but amidst all the good times we spent together, I discovered that this "uneducated man" had a sensitive side, a breadth and depth of thought and feeling I'd never suspected.

Jerry didn't conform to my shallow first impressions but was genuinely interested in spiritual things and loved to pray. Rather than going out for a fancy dinner or seeing a show, for example, he asked to spend our first Valentine's Day together at the seminary. He was curious about what happened at such a school. He met me in class at 7:30 a.m. sharp and stayed the full day, engaged with other students, talked with professors, and sat in on my classes. None of my classmates had ever experienced anything like it. At dinner that night, we sat at the bar, the only open spot in the restaurant, when he handed me a friendly Valentine...and then had the audacity to ask me what kind of man I would consider marrying!

"A pastor," I fired back.

"NO! NO! NO!" Pounding his fist on the bar in mock anger he said, "There can't be two of you in one family!"

Before earning a master's in divinity, Luther Seminary required all students to spend the third academic year of their programs interning in a church. Most stayed close to home serving churches in small towns in Minnesota, Wisconsin, Iowa, and the Dakotas. I had my sights set farther off the beaten path. In weighing the pros and cons of different sites, I came up with four essential criteria: First, the church had to be located somewhere easily accessible and fun for my boys and their families to visit. That ruled out the familiar rolling hills and hamlets of the rural Midwest. Second, the internship had to enrich and expand my horizons as a future Christian leader; third the experience had to offer both visibility and responsibility. Finally, it had to satisfy my lifelong wanderlust to be somewhere I could meet new and different kinds of people and gain life- and faith-expanding experiences.

After sifting through a long list of possibilities, I found the perfect fit: Community Lutheran Church in Las Vegas, Nevada. Not only did it satisfy all three criteria, but it also gave me the opportunity to gain experience in a large church setting. *This was it*, I thought, *the place I was meant to be.*

On my way to interview with the recruiter, I came to a stoplight, and as I waited for the light to change, an exchange between two fellow students popped my balloon. Community Lutheran decided against offering an internship that year, one informed the other. Not only was I disappointed at the lost opportunity, but I didn't have a backup plan. Although students were encouraged to interview with five or six churches, my heart was so set on Community Lutheran I hadn't signed up to interview with any others. I'd packed my mind and heart in a suitcase bound for Vegas with no plan B.

Several weeks later, standing at that same stoplight waiting to cross that same street, another conversation intervened. "Hey, did you hear Las Vegas is in town?" one student asked the other. I turned right around and made a beeline back to the administration building.

A member of the Community Lutheran congregation dying of cancer believed so strongly that the church *did* need an intern that he personally funded the position and flew Pastor Ray Christensen to Minnesota to interview prospective candidates. The morning he arrived, I was his first interview. He then called me back again at six o'clock that evening for a second conversation, after which he offered me the internship.

A true visionary genius, Christensen had founded Community Lutheran Church in 1972, and it became a huge success—a Lutheran equivalent of Robert Schuler's Crystal Cathedral. Under his leadership, Community Lutheran developed trail-blazing new programs later adopted by other Lutheran churches nationwide. The opportunity to work with and learn from his experience would be unique. Everything was falling into place perfectly.

I was excited about the adventure ahead, but also daunted by the challenge of leaving family and friends behind. *It's hard to leave the nest,* I wrote in my journal, *but I'm going to Vegas by Your design and the future looks very challenging. Ray described me as "a strong, gifted woman who can bring a lot to our staff." Now I'm wondering if I can, and if it's more than I can accomplish. Did I say too much—will they expect me as a student or a staff person? I try to picture myself in the position, and the image is very hazy—the possibility of becoming a pastor still exists in my dreams, where it's safe and far away. Yet taking responsibility and a position, however, has not taken on any substantial form. My fears are lessened by the*

knowledge that You wait for me at every turn and will nourish me as You always have.

Adding to my concern about meeting expectations was the question of Jerry. Where did he fit as I launched into ministry? He and I had only been dating ten months before the internship began, and I had to start getting settled in Las Vegas right away. Was this to be a parting of the ways or an opportunity to get closer? I was concerned that just as I was about to spread my wings and fly, the demands of our relationship might somehow sabotage my dreams. Once again, it was confusing—everything was moving so fast. Could I be there for Jerry and keep my commitment to serving God?

Lord Jesus, I journaled, *what am I to do about Jerry? Have You sent him into my life as a companion, a future mate, or a test of my loyalty? I could easily fall in love—maybe am already. It's so different from Bob that I can't compare the feelings, the qualities, and virtues Jerry bears; they all add up to an incredible man. Yet I do not know what role his faith plays or is to play in this relationship. I would call him a godly man in so many ways—but his church relations make me nervous. And he has not spoken of You with love and commitment. Do men speak that way? Should I be satisfied that he doesn't speak negatively or skeptically?*

Finding myself once again at a major change point, I pleaded with God for answers. *What do You have in mind for us? What kind of man would make a good husband for me, especially considering ministry? My question remains simply: Will I be a better pastor/servant if I stay single?* Again, God didn't tip His hand but left me waiting in the dark.

REFLECTION

I was so enchanted with the opening quote of this chapter the year I turned fifty that every journal for the next twenty years had it recorded. That was the year my first husband died, and life changed dramatically. All at once, "dreams and endeavors" became possible, and I wasted little time redesigning life on my own terms.

But God's dream for me was beyond my imagination—an impossible reality that I am now sitting in as I write this. I am surprised every day with the enormity of His plan for me that far exceeded anything I could have possibly envisioned. Trusting God to bring surprises is getting to be a necessity.

DISCUSSION

He never wastes anything in His creation or in your experiences when you learn to look through His eyes.

1. Have you ever considered that the scenes of your life serve a story much bigger than your own?

2. Have you ever lived through events that were change points or defining moments that God can use in the future?

ACTION

I encourage you to dream and endeavor to live a life imagined. Stop trying to figure out what God wants you to do. His dreams are too big for us to conceive.

1. Start where you are, journal your ideas and dreams, and risk advancing confidently in that direction.

2. I was challenged to keep a running list of one hundred goals by a friend of mine so that I could recognize a goal when it came toward me. How about creating a list of dreams, goals, projects, small and great—from cleaning a closet to riding in a yellow submarine? It is a lot of fun to be able to cross things off your list.

CHAPTER TEN

LEAVING LAS VEGAS

"There ain't no way you can hold onto something that wants to go, you understand? You can only love what you got while you got it."[11]

—KATE DICAMILLO

The summer before leaving for Las Vegas, Jerry asked me to marry him. I didn't hesitate and we made all the plans and reservations, expecting a huge event since it involved two popular Waconia families of seven sons. We planned for the boys to travel to Las Vegas for a week of celebration before the wedding. The church welcomed us both with great loving outreach.

I was finally in the right place, at the right time, doing the right thing for the right reasons. As a pastoral intern at one

---

11 Kate DiCamillo, *Because of Winn-Dixie* (Somerville, MA: Candlewick Press, 2009).

of the largest and most influential Lutheran churches in the United States, I had a rare opportunity to test my pastoring potential on a superhighway rather than a back road. That it all came about so improbably added an air of mystery to the calling. Only God could have perfectly matched my desire to work with an innovative staff engaged in multiple ministries with the needs of a congregation positioned in such a culturally supercharged arena.

Community Lutheran was a leader in creative ministry. To accommodate the large and diverse crowd of worshipers (one-third Air Force base; one-third Las Vegas citizens, musicians, and artists; and one-third transplants from other states), the church held five services every Sunday, each with a different style of worship. From rap and country to classical and modern, performers combined music with visual arts to create meaningful worship experiences. In addition to three full-time pastors, the church employed a full-time psychologist and nine secretaries. But there was more. Community Lutheran also operated a publishing company, large kitchens staffed with professional chefs, a preschool, and a community outreach offering multiple resources and services. Working in such a dynamic environment made my head spin!

The internship matched perfectly with my experience and goals and the church's immediate needs. "Everything you touch turns to gold," church leaders happily reported. As the only woman pastor, I found my place and confirmed my calling. I was encouraged and able to introduce new programming that impacted people's lives. I felt more fulfilled than ever.

On the evening of December 26, 1995, Jerry and I were waiting for our seven sons and their families to arrive. The phone rang. It was Tyson calling from the Carver County Jail in Minnesota. There had been an accident earlier that evening, he said in fits and starts as he related the heartbreaking story. He and his lifetime friend, Jonathon, while four-wheeling on Lake Waconia on a very dark night struck an ice ridge at full throttle, sending both flying off the ATV and onto the ice. While Tyson suffered only minor cuts and bruises, Jonathon was rushed to Hennepin County Medical Center and later died from his injuries.

"I was driving, Mom," Tyson said in a voice wracked with guilt.

Tyson and Jonathan had been close friends since second grade, when they began riding bikes together and later four-wheelers and motorcycles as teens. Though parting ways after high school, the two kept in touch. Jonathan enlisted in the military, while Tyson used his skilled machinist's degree to land a job in a small-engine repair shop. Jonathan was home on leave for the holidays and hadn't seen Tyson since high school graduation in June 1993.

The day after Christmas, the boys joined some old high school friends for an evening of ice fishing, playing darts, and root beer shots (though Tyson hadn't touched alcohol since getting sober in 1992). They decided to quit for supper, and the two friends headed home to take the truck uptown for burgers. But on opening the garage door, they both spied the four-wheeler parked by the truck.

"We wore the biggest grins on our faces," Tyson later recounted, as they hopped on the four-wheeler "for old time's sake" and set off across the lake to the restaurant. Tyson was driving, Jonathan in back.

It was an especially dark night as they turned onto what they thought was the access road that wound around the little village of five hundred ice fish houses on Lake Waconia. Unfortunately, a neighbor had plowed a private access road off the main road to get to his skating rink, and in the darkness, Tyson gunned the engine and hit the ice ridge around the rink. They both flew off the bike and onto the ice. Tyson was banged up, but Jonathon died from a brain injury. When police arrived, Tyson told them he'd been driving and voluntarily took a Breathalyzer test that showed his blood alcohol to be above the legal limit. He was immediately taken into custody and locked in the jail when he called me. I called Kyle to get him released.

It was a slow news week when we got back home and saw the accident highlighted in the media. The headline, "Man Kills Best Friend" was an attention grabber. The tragedy also coincided with a recently released report showing that Carver County had more alcohol-related vehicle deaths than any other county in Minnesota. Because Tyson had been drinking underage (he was twenty at the time of the accident, and the drinking age in Minnesota was twenty-one), the county prosecutor wanted to send a message. He sought the maximum sentence of seven years in prison. Considering this tragic homecoming, it seemed impossible to think about the wedding.

Jonathon's parents didn't blame Tyson and, in fact, asked me to design their son's funeral with Tyson as a pallbearer and me presiding at his service. The whole community attended with many of the same guests invited to the wedding. January 20, 1996, two days after the funeral, Jerry and I exchanged vows, swearing before God to love and care for each other till death do us part. We then celebrated with a huge dinner-dance until the early hours. Neither of us suspected how quickly the "do us part "was to be.

Jerry left for the honeymoon we'd planned with friends in California, and I stayed with Tyson that next week before returning to Las Vegas. The ice storm that occurred the weekend of our wedding knocked out the power, so the house was cold and dark when we arrived. We built a fire in the fireplace, and I sat down beside Tyson.

"Mom," he agonizingly began, "I should be the one that died. It's all my fault. I'm always the one who gets in trouble."

"I don't know why Jonathan died," I said, "but it's really important for you to know there's a reason you're still here and Jonathan is with the Lord. He's safe and much more alive than you or I are right now." I didn't know what was going to happen, I told him, but urged patience. "Remember, your name is Tyson, a 'gift of Jehovah,'" I said. "Somehow, God is creating you as an unusual gift, making you someone people want to listen to because you've learned some hard things in life that most people don't understand. All I know is that God's doing something miraculous, and you don't want to miss it." That was the word of hope he needed for his future. And we settled into the darkness in the wonder of it all.

We arranged for a lawyer to walk us through the details of the legal process and got Tyson settled at Kyle's home. Meanwhile, a deluge of letters and phone calls from the neighborhood began swamping the prosecutor's desk.

"This kid is too good to be true," the attorney told a leader in Waconia. "Go anywhere and ask anyone you want. Use your own resources and you will find he is from a good family and is a fine young man." Though Tyson's fate remained uncertain through that fall, the Waconia community's response gave us hope.

Impressed by the vast outpouring of affection, the prosecutor changed course and became Tyson's advocate! Instead of the maximum sentence of seven years in prison previously sought, he and the judge made a deal whereby Tyson would pay a small fine and spend three years on probation working in the county garages as a mechanic. They later reduced his sentence to one year after mechanics raved about Tyson's attitude and the quality of workmanship on their trucks._

Back in Las Vegas, Jerry and I lived in a little condo that became our first home. My colleagues and the Community Lutheran family surrounded us with loving attention. For about a month and a half, life was back on track. Then in March 1996, two months after the wedding, Jerry came home one day and said, "I don't feel so good, and I don't think it's the flu." He took the next flight back to Waconia to see his doctor on a Tuesday, and I followed on Wednesday. Doctors confirmed that a melanoma, treated nine years earlier, had spread, and he needed immediate chemotherapy. The prognosis was dire.

Before resigning my internship to be with Jerry, I flew back to Las Vegas to give one last sermon. After the service, a line of people formed to thank me for the message and bless me on my way. Before shaking hands, a tall gentleman whom I'd never met before paused and handed me a rock. I thanked him for the souvenir from Las Vegas to take back home.

"Oh, no," he said, "that isn't it. I was there when the Berlin Wall came down. I want to give you one of the two pieces of the wall I picked up," he said, "because you've changed my life."

Despite losing the dream of being a pastor, I'd never felt so honored and restored. Community Lutheran's leaders could not have been more generous or understanding. They gave me a full year's credit for my internship and asked me to consider returning as a member of the staff.

I have kept that rock on a shelf in my private living space at the Blessing House as a reminder that even though my time there was brief, I did make a difference in people's lives. Whenever I found myself feeling bitter about having my dream snatched away again, I would hold that rock to restore my perspective. It also reminded me that in the realm of the eternal, the blessings I received at Community Lutheran Church were the confirmation of my calling that far outweighed the frustrations of ambition.

After leaving Las Vegas and returning to Minnesota, the community of friends and our extended family did all they could to make Jerry's last months as joyful as possible. Every night, our blended family of seven sons, wives, and grandchildren gathered for the evening meal, games, and companionship. Our bedroom became a hospital room where his many friends could visit and pray for Jerry and the hospital staff that kept him alive. As his health failed in the final weeks, Jerry asked to have his feeding tubes removed, while keeping the pain mitigation in place. Thus began a one-week vigil ending in a last night of loving celebration where, one by one, he invited each of his sons, daughters-in-law, and grandchildren to sit on his bed while he blessed them with affirmations, told stories, and gave each a kiss goodnight. It was a surprisingly joyful evening of stories, jokes, and laughter. To the very end, he remained amazingly alive.

The next morning, Jerry died in my arms, the memory of our first kiss still fresh in my memory as I kissed him goodbye. The love story that began with a kiss meant for a lifetime, also ended with a kiss. He died a good death.

The news spread quickly, and within a couple hours the community began gathering for an old-fashioned wake. Jerry laid in the bed until three o'clock that afternoon when the hearse arrived, so friends could spend as much time as possible with him. The party continued late into the next morning, full of stories, tears, food, drinks, and of course, cards. The funeral was again a community affair, with many of the same guests at our wedding returning to attend the funeral. Jerry's sons spoke of their father, and the grandchildren, who sang his favorite song from *The Lion King* at our wedding, sang a last goodbye.

The loss was staggering on many levels. I'd come so close to having all my hopes and dreams fulfilled after years of stagnation. Now the gift of a loving husband and partner was snatched away, and my future career faded into memory. Community Lutheran offered me a full-time position in Las Vegas, but I had little left to give and two families hurting in Waconia.

A month later, I collapsed in despair. The anger Jerry had sensed inside of me, which I didn't know was there, erupted like a volcano. My rage against God was bottomless.

"I would scratch Your eyes out if I could get to You!" I screamed at Him.

"I made Myself available," He answered back.

In the deep, black silence there came a vision in the middle of the day. I saw myself at the whipping post where Christ was scourged and picked up a bloody whip and began lashing the One who called Himself God with all my might.

"This is what I think of You, God," I heard myself shout in anger. The fury inside me overflowed. "I've loved You my whole life and was glad to serve You in obedience to Your Word and become a servant to others by denying myself. This is the thanks I get! What's the matter? Did I enjoy it too much?"

Then covered with His blood, the Spirit took me to the cross where Jesus was hanging. Still engulfed in murderous rage, I picked up a hammer and began nailing His feet to the wooden beam. Through my hate-filled eyes, I looked up and saw Him looking down at me from the cross with eyes of love! I was speechless.

Out of my heart's jagged walls poured the black sludge of resentment over unanswered prayers, frustrated dreams, and dying husbands. I experienced the malignant hatred human beings feel toward a God who seems to abandon us, thwart our plans, and rain down injustice.

If I were God, I thought, *I would never have done what He did to me after fifty years of loyal service!* When the dam finally broke, I wept my heart dry. It was then the revelation that Jesus didn't die to redeem us just from what we know of ourselves, but even more of what we don't know about those deep hidden places.

I spent the next weeks in silence trying to make sense of what happened. The Holy Spirit had soothed the sharp edges of my heart with a healing balm.

"I don't get it," I said from my rocking chair in the living room. "I'm down here while You sit high on Your throne seeing what I can't see. I don't understand why Jerry had to die. You gave me a poisoned apple, a Trojan Horse full of deceit, a beautiful package filled with dead men's bones. I do not understand Your ways!"

At that moment, God gave me another live vision of myself getting out of my rocking chair and opening the front door. On the other side was an enormous, regal Cheshire Cat preening himself, very proud of the gift he had laid at my feet, a dead bird. It made me wonder, *What does this cat know that I don't—that his finest gift is a dead bird?* Then came the revelation. God's greatest gift to us was not the powerful Jesus that walked on water, healed the sick, and raised the dead, but that bloody corpse hanging on the cross, Christ crucified.

Only then did the truth sink in. It wasn't the life of Jerry that was God's greatest gift but his death! The gift of Jerry did not end with his life but would continue beyond the grave. As that knowledge slowly sank in, the blackness filling my soul by so many disappointments and setbacks began to fade. Instead of going nowhere, I was NOW HERE, fully present, and grateful for this strange gift that I had yet to open. I didn't yet understand why, but I was at peace.

I returned to finish seminary in January, graduating with my class but exhausted by the strain of pacing a four-year program into three years, with two husbands' deaths as bookends. Next came the four-hour interview with seminary leaders to determine if I should be ordained. I was approved with a final prophetic comment by a head professor. "Your congregations are going to love you, but the other pastors are not."

That insight helped me decide to accept an offer to work as an apologist for Dr. Don Bierle's HIS Ministries. I liked the freedom of working in many kinds of churches in an innovative teaching capacity where I didn't have to worry about threatening the other pastors. I watched many people give their lives to Christ for the first time when they discovered that the Bible is true, accurate, and historical. They had sat in the pews for years doubting the veracity of the Word of God, and now they were excited to be Christians.

During those years, I began receiving phone calls from women who said someone told them they should contact me. They were a diverse group who lived all over the Twin Cities and worked in many capacities in schools, television, government, missions, finance, and business. I reserved a table for twelve at one of St. Paul's historic hotels and watched as they all entered looking a little lost. Two hours later, we had only just begun getting acquainted with our stories and decided to finish the following week at my home on Lake Waconia. The question we yet had to answer was, "What was God up to in this unusual setting of women who had never met and yet been summoned?" For the next several years, friendships grew deeply as sisters who called ourselves the daughters of Issachar (after the description in First Chronicles 12:32), for the tribe who understood the times and knew what to do. Our paths continued to cross and enrich one another's callings.

I, personally, was redirected in my ministry by Rev. Dawn Lundgren, an evangelist-prophet. She invited me to travel as a teaching pastor with her and Pastor Barbara Mitchell, who directed well-health clinics. The three of us traveled Africa, the Philippines, Turkey, Israel, and the West Bank between 1999 and 2008, where I experienced the worldwide church. I was also ordained in the Sea of Galilee after my adult baptism. We moved in cultures tourists rarely experience, and I was stunned with the power of the gospel and the love of God in the poorest of places. I was privileged to see miracles, deal with witchcraft, be in dangerous places, and discover the power of the Holy Spirit directing, warning, and guarding us as we moved through difficult days. I was able to see the world with God's eyes and experience sights most people never would be exposed to. We treated ourselves to several safari adventures and returned with unique treasures from all the countries.

In 2007 I was invited to join Operation Mobilization and travel into northern India and work with the Dalits deemed "the untouchables." We held training conferences with the pastors of this indigenous community and visited villages, encouraging the beautiful families whose lives were being changed by the gospel and the work of the Dalit Freedom Network. Those churches brought life and hope through education, job training, and ministry in the bleakest of communities.

When I left Las Vegas discouraged with the loss of any professional ministry, I had no idea God was preparing glorious years of adventure, travel, and stunning vistas of His power. It was also during this period that I began reconsidering the possibility of transforming my 1950s rambler on Lakeview Terrace into a teaching/gathering center for people seeking a deeper life in the Spirit. As my creative juices began flowing in this direction, new ideas and insights from my travels captured my imagination.

Though my life is rooted in the spiritual domain, I am also fascinated with the design, shapes, patinas, curves, and lines of the physical realm. I am drawn to organic colors, certain kinds of chairs, fabrics, and art garnered from both books I've collected and countries I've traveled. I can't resist the antique, the classical, the stained glass and large art pieces that tell a story. I came to understand why I had collected and filed away pictures of furniture, fabric, and window coverings; images of plants and pieces of wood, metal, and rock; wall arrangements; and so on.

I opened my files, laid out all their contents on the floor, and began looking for patterns and common themes. Creating indoor and outdoor spaces as rooms for people to dream, think, converse, and imagine new ways of life. I could visualize the pathways and structures, the scenes and nature of space that could help them experience the love of God. A vision of spaces pulsing with story and meaning manifested in material form continued to emerge. I finally recognized the calling to my own home mission.

I opened the remodeled house to the public in 1997. As word got around, people started dropping by to visit—first it was neighbors, then they started bringing friends and people from their churches.

One day in January 2000, I happened to notice a posting on the bulletin board announcing the start-up of a new church, Waterbrooke Community Fellowship. Something about the timing and description of the church caught my eye. So, I contacted the leaders of Waterbrooke and became a founding member. It is a rare experience to be on the ground floor of a new church. Creating, designing, planning, and building always satisfied my entrepreneurial spirit. I never realized then that I'd need to draw on all that training and experience when the time came to build the Blessing House.

REFLECTION

Things that make the deepest impression come from thrift stores, garage sales, or antique stores. Though I may lack the words to describe these strange attractions, I believe they radiate "at-home-ness." These physical bits and pieces have power to reach deep into our souls and bring a smile, a tear, a memory. It is in their intrinsic value, their heart connection, that makes these things beautiful.

Our lives are so much richer when the objects placed in our surroundings tell a story that is meaningful to us. Our children and grandchildren need to know these stories because in them God speaks of relationships, adventures, marvels, and love. Our lives are trophies of His grace and mercy, and the things in our lives often speak of those stories. I know no better way to connect generations of family ties than sharing our lives through story objects. Our stories matter: our victories and defeats have meaning because they keep us close to each other and our Maker. God made us for story—not decrees and councils and rules. Perhaps you would like to bring such an object to your study group and share its meaning.

DISCUSSION

What does it mean to "decorate" a home? The verb decorate comes from the Latin root "décor," meaning "to make beautiful." People take great pride in decorating their homes and sometimes spend great sums to replicate displays on showroom floors. These interiors may be generically attractive, but they often lack any sense of history and story.

There is another way to think about our homes—as flourishing expressions of our deepest values that invite others into our story. My joy is to make a home that is comfortable, useful for conversation, and an invitation to rest a while. Discuss ideas of how you would like your home to reflect you.

ACTION

1. Make a collage. Gather up a bundle of old magazines, a pair of scissors, a large piece of construction paper, and some glue or rubber cement. As you slowly page through the magazines, stop to notice the images that catch your eye and tug at your heart. Cut out pictures you find particularly compelling and try different ways of arranging

them on the paper. Once again, notice the connections and associations you love the most that stir your soul and reflect your values, hopes, aspirations. Do you see any themes, patterns, or stories emerging from the images?

2. Use your collage as a prompt to tell a story about yourself. Consider writing down this story and sharing it with others. Reflect on these experiences. Did anything you learned about yourself come as a surprise? Were there any unexpected insights?

3. What steps could you take right now to better align the proddings of your heart with the material world around you?

4. Take an artist's holiday. Get acquainted with yourself and what you like. Ask yourself, "What object speaks to me or stirs memories, dreams, or desires?" Visit new stores—at first—and make a note of how you feel inside. Then go into secondhand places, thrift stores, antique malls, yard sales, and look for stories in the objects you are drawn to examine more closely. Start homing in on your authentic likes and dislikes, moving away from the fashions and lifestyle trends of the moment.

CHAPTER ELEVEN

LIFE ON THE LINE

"What kind of person
What kind of life
What kind of love
Brings the friend of a brother
Or the friend of a stepbrother
Or the friend of a stepbrother's wife
Into a line
That, as we stepped into the building
Was still getting longer
Out the door
Down the sidewalk
And now across the road."
—SUE STAGG, "THE LINE"[12]

12 Sue Stagg, "The Line." Used by permission.

It was Tyson's last race of the season, and the boisterous capacity crowd at the Brainerd International Speedway was expecting a good one. As the riders pulled their motorcycles to the starting line and revved their engines, spectators in the stands roared approval. Many were undoubtedly grateful for the respite from bad news. For a little while at least, they could let off steam and detach from the 9/11 national tragedy they had watched unfolding on their televisions four days earlier.

At twenty-six, Tyson had accomplished a lot in his rookie year on the motorcycle racing circuit. More than his racing skills, I was proud of the character and integrity he'd developed in overcoming a series of personal struggles and setbacks from an early age—his drug use at age twelve, his father's death from alcoholism at age seventeen, and his best friend's tragic death at age twenty. After reentering treatment for the second time, Tyson's life began looking up.

He lived in Crosslake, Minnesota, with Heather and their son, Ghage, on Dew Drop Lake to be near the racing scene in Brainerd and open his first business, Berg's Motor Sports. He met Dave Schmallenburg and began racing under his team, moving to expert class within one year. The next year, Dave asked Tyson to partner in their businesses because he had so much respect for Tyson's expertise with engines and his racing accomplishments. Racing gave Tyson enormous adrenaline he craved in an arena where he could focus all his natural gifts. His capacity for life and relationships drew many people to him.

It was the last race of the season, and many old friends were there from the Twin Cities, but I was not. I was at home helping Kyle and Amy move into their new home when we got the call.

"There has been a bad accident. I think you had better come up here," said one of his best friends.

Roadracing World reported,

> "It happened early in the race on the first turn of the first lap of the last race of the season. First-year CRA Expert racer Tyson Berger, 26, was killed in a racing accident at Brainerd International Speedway in Brainerd, Minnesota, on Saturday, September 15, 2001. Berger crashed his Suzuki SV650 in a three-bike-pile-up in Turn One on the first lap of the Super Twins race. According to CRA President Eddie Karow, Berger was pronounced Dead on Arrival at the local hospital with spinal cord injuries. Karow told *Roadracing World* Tuesday, September 18, the two other riders involved in the accident suffered non-life-threatening injuries. "This was the last event of the year," said an emotionally drained Karow. "Everyone wanted to go out on a good note. Unfortunately, we lost Tyson."

I remember the feeling as if I were in an airplane speeding down the runway as we traveled those 150 miles not knowing what had happened. Our phone calls gave us no more information until the control tower reported Tyson had died and had been taken back to the Hennepin County Coroner. That very moment I was lifted over *terra firma*, catching my breath like one does in a plane. Every plane ride since brings back that haunting reality, and I am back in the car hearing the words, "Tyson died." In fact, I was airborne for a year. People came for visits, but they could never join me in that suspended world in which I alone existed. The plane finally landed in a "yellowed wood" with another chance to choose a "road less taken."[13]

The Hennepin County coroner, Janice DeAnatagio, called to ask if we would be willing to donate Tyson's body to the crisis in New York. "He had the most perfect body I have ever seen," she said. "There was not an ounce of fat on him. He was beautiful." They later reported that forty lives were affected by all his parts, inside and out. His death saved many people, and he left behind a five-week-old son, now twenty-one, who is the exact image of Tyson. Even as the Lord takes away, He gives and gives and gives. This is a faith statement that can take a long time to accept.

Many people poured into Waconia to attend the reviewal, including sixty motorcyclists from the five-state area. The line outside Johnson Funeral Home kept growing as people came to be with us. Men broke down at the casket, stories were told of how he was an amazing gift, and people wrote poems about him. One woman, stunned with the number of people arriving, wrote a poem as she waited called "The Line," which is partially included at the beginning of this chapter.

"Did you ever meet him?" I asked as she approached me.

"Not really," she answered.

---

13 10 Robert Frost, "The Road Not Taken" (Mineola, NY: Dover Publications, 1926).

"Oh, you should have known him. I loved him so much."

She said nothing and moved on. But within a week, she sent me a gift of the poem she wrote while standing in that long line. The poet saw a physical manifestation of the way Tyson's love touched so many lives. It was what he did and who he was that made the line so long. I know the Lord loved the way he raced the wind, but even more the way he connected with everyone who came into his presence. It didn't matter if it was 2:00 a.m. when a visitor saw the light on in the garage, Tyson always welcomed them.

I couldn't help remembering the night I sat with Tyson by the fireside, and I spoke prophetically about his name meaning "Gift of Jehovah" and that God was going to use him to bless many people. And at the reviewal and funeral service, I was able to hear the stories of his influence.

For all the pain and difficulty he experienced in his short life, no one lived larger than Tyson. He truly lived out the meaning of his name. He and I shared the same kindred spirit that got both of us in trouble as teenagers. God took both of us to the end of that life and repurposed our spirits to be useful in His hands.

From an early age, Tyson was a whirling dervish. His father called him "Tigger" after the joyful, energetic character from Winnie the Pooh. He always thought he was the same age as his brothers, and there wasn't anything he couldn't do. He radiated trouble. He ended up in the hospital many times—swallowed a plastic piece as a one-year-old, was hit by a car on his bike at age five, had both shoulders operated on from racing, and was brought home by police for infractions. Of the three boys, Tyson was most overtly affected by the emotional tensions and genetic vulnerabilities as was his father. Not only did he witness Bob's last days, but he bore the brunt of his mood swings and black-and-white thinking. Amidst the chaos and desperation, Tyson got lost in the shuffle.

Nothing cut my heart more deeply than Tyson's death. If it hadn't been for Jerry's death that had emptied me of so much anger, I don't know if I would have come out of the tailspin. It stripped away all my defenses, demolished every idol. There was no way around the pain of loss, no "best face" to put on his death. It shredded any illusion of a world I could count on to be safe or predictable.

Tyson's death revealed the limits of my faith. I still clung to the things of this world for safety, meaning, and value. I was coming to a crossroads where I'd have to choose between giving all my life, holding nothing back, to God or drown in my own sorrow. I had learned the hard way that everything is vulnerable to loss. I didn't know exactly what that meant at first, but there was no evading the consequences of this change point. Within seven years, I had lost two husbands in their fifties, ravaged by disease, and a son in his twenties, who died perfect. All were change points that altered the trajectory of my life in different ways. Seven is the number of completion, and I wondered if the rest of my life would be wide enough to encapsulate all that pain in some indescribable way I could not imagine at that time.

Without the necessity of rediscovering myself after Bob's death, I might have never summoned the strength to follow my heart and become the person God created me to be. Without the inner healing following Jerry's death, I couldn't have survived the heartbreak of losing Tyson. And without the agony of losing Tyson, I never would have felt compelled to give all that was left of my life back into the hands of God.

It took time to discern God's ways of helping me heal from this tragedy, but when it did, the guidance was clear. Tyson's death set me on the path to become a Steward.

Bob's death set me free.
Jerry's death a gift from Thee,
Tyson's death, not about me.

REFLECTION

God burns away all attachments to anything but Him...which means learning to live the eternal life (*zoe*) now. The deepest lesson that emerged from Tyson's death was the clarity about eternal life. I had always thought of it as life after death and a life that was waiting for me. But *zoe* encompasses all of life for the Christian. Learning to live in eternal life *now* is the gift God gives us through the Holy Spirit.

DISCUSSION

Once you realize everything is fallible, can be taken in a minute, and not meant to stay here, the reality is haunting because you truly have no control over life events. That is when you seek a greater reality that is found only in the Word of God, and the desire for a life that is connected to the eternal realm begins to grow. It takes practice to live in time and space as an "eternal one."

Knowing this, how does that change your life—the way you think about the past and how you perceive what your future can be? You will begin to understand that you're from a different realm with different rules, principles, powers, and wisdom. You will perceive what is going on around you differently, knowing that you are an eternal one whose future has been secured by the Lord.

ACTION

Begin to read again the Word of God searching for all it has to say about eternal life and the eternal realm. For instance, what does it mean to have abundant life? John 10:10 explains this: "But I came that they might have, keep, and constantly retain a vitality, gusto, vigor, and zest for living those springs from deep inside. I came that they might embrace this unrivaled, unequaled, matchless, incomparable, richly loaded, and overflowing life to the ultimate maximum."[14]

Here are more passages that refer to *zoe* as the life force of God:

John 1:4
John 3:16
John 5:26
Romans 6:23
1 John 1:1–4

14 Rick Renner, *Sparkling Gems from the Greek Vol. 1: 365 Greek Word Studies for Every Day of the Year to Sharpen Your Understanding of God's Word* (Tulsa, OK: Teach All Nations, 2003).

As you are living in *zoe*, you are learning to live in the NOW where God is fully present. You will know when you have stepped out of the NOW because the enemy brings worry, fear, distrust, unforgiveness, anger—all the things in life that consume and take you down. Learning to stay in the NOW is a powerful way to live because God is always a NOW God.

CHAPTER TWELVE

SWITCHING KINGDOMS

***"The call to follow Christ is a call to adventure— inconvenient, imperious, and irresistible."*[15]**

—MALCOLM MUGGERIDGE

The radiance of the early sun fell on perfectly still waters as I sipped my morning coffee. Yes! A perfect day for an outing with the Shady Ladies on Lake Waconia. They hadn't known each other more than a few months and were still getting acquainted. All single, in their forties, beautiful and talented women who knew tragedy and heartache. Our stories brought each of us to seek shelter under the shadow of the Most High God, so I named them "the Shady Ladies" from Psalm 17:8, where the psalmist asks God to be able to hide in the shadow of His wings.

---

15 Malcolm Muggeridge, *The End of Christendom* (Grand Rapids, MI: Wm B. Erdman Publishing Co, 1980), 56.

They all arrived with drinks and snacks for the pontoon ride. As I slowly guided the boat through the gentle waves around Coney Island, I spied my island destination with the great rope swing attached to a tall oak, reachable only by a ladder up to a two-story platform. I was turning sixty in a few months, and the siren song of the rope swing was handing me an invitation to my yearly risk! After the deaths of my husbands, I determined to do something each year I'd never done before. It is my contention that a person should take one risk a year just to stay young and alive. Though I'd never jumped from the rope swing before, I, being the eldest, challenged the ladies to join me. I cut the engine and dove into the water. None of the ladies joined me, preferring to stay dry.

As I climbed the steep wooden ladder to the platform, I experienced déjà vu about the backward high dive I did in college. It took three giant steps and a leap off the platform to reach the rope and propel over the lake.

One. Two. Threeeee! I flew, plunging into the cool waters. As I surfaced, I watched several of them jump off the boat and swim for the shore, not to be outdone by an "old lady." No one will forget that day for several reasons. The risk, the story, the long sunny afternoon, and the rich night of conversation when hearts were open went till 3:00 a.m.

I know that what goes on in my house helps many people, I wrote in my journal. *Something wonderful is stirring.* The purpose of remodeling and opening the home on Lakeview Terrace to make a

Christ-centered life real for others was meeting important needs unmet by other religious organizations and churches. It was exciting to see the fulfillment of this dream come true over the last ten years. A large part of my identity had been wrapped up in being prepared and willing to meet people's need of belonging. I loved serving in this role and found it energizing because it required all my skills and gifts.

To use my home and belongings was a thrill. Even more so was to offer classes, special events, training in art and health and personal growth. I loved all the creative aspects of establishing the house on Lakeview Terrace as a place of celebration, study, rest, and prayer.

Yet something more kept surfacing. I found myself in a familiar place of dissatisfaction, boredom, restlessness. For all the success I was experiencing, part of me wanted to scrap the whole thing and start something new. I felt stuck in maintaining something. I am much happier to move forward into a new idea that takes a greater faith and requires a different kind of leadership.

Tyson's death reminded me how tenuous life really is. Anything can be taken, and my hold on life could not stop it. Slowly I began to reopen the future. Classes resumed, people drifted in and out, I gave speeches about the difference between being nowhere and returning to a place called NOW HERE. I could tell the story about what the journey of life and death and the return to life had taught me.

Tyson's death had brought me to the end of my plans. That is when God asked me, "What if you gave everything back to Me I've ever given you?"

I love what-if questions, but God's question took me a long time to answer. What if I gave everything back to Him and virtually owned nothing? I would need to become a Steward of the Lord's possessions, owning nothing yet possessing everything. For one year I blogged, asking what it meant to be a Steward, owning nothing.

God had allowed me many years of creative, expanding life with enough love, beauty, children, and friends for several lifetimes. I lived through tragic disaster, discouragement, broken promises, pain, and loss. Three deaths in seven years haunted me. I learned the height and depth of the human experience, yet at this point of success, I still felt unfinished. I couldn't shake the feeling that God had a new assignment for me, and it had something to do with expanding the reach of the Lakeview Terrace Blessing House.

I began to daydream of possibilities of expansion to serve more people. The lack of parking space in a neighborhood was a problem and limited the number of people who could take advantage of the programs and events. I thought of purchasing the neighbors' homes that had entered the market recently, but they were too expensive, and a compound would not be welcomed by the neighbors. My sons suggested buying a farm on the outskirts of town, but I wanted a home in a neighborhood, not a retreat center.

Should I be taking account of my age? I wrote in my journal. *Why would I want to build when I already had a lovely home and lifestyle? Yet, such a project stirs my imagination and my heart pumps a little faster. If money were no issue and time of no consequence, what other ways might I help create more space for God to work?*

I began to dream and scheme without filtering my thoughts through the "real world" resistance by which every new idea is judged. A new vision began forming in my mind, the dream of an intentionally designed, creative living center filled with beautiful spaces for God to work in both the depths and the shallows of our lives.

- A place that filled the God-shaped void in so many lives
- A place to connect with God in everyday ways
- A place of joy that welcomed the stranger to experience God's peace and love directly through the warmth and comforts of a place that felt like home
- A refuge, a haven, a place where matter and spirit come together.

It would be open where anyone could go for reflection and meditation with ongoing classes, prayer, and worship at its center. This enclosed space, outside the distracted, materialistic noise where small things mattered, like a cup of coffee and conversation, a quiet place to read, a garden, a misty bog to walk alongside, or a lake to sit and stare at for no apparent reason.

This sacred place would transcend denominations, dogma, creeds, where anyone could go to be embraced by God, not by words alone, but by seeing for themselves the very thing that made the early Christians so attractive. Today, people want and need the same things they wanted and needed back then—a heart free to give and receive love without fear and homes who welcomed them.

From these early wonderings, a different version of a blessing house—one designed and built expressly for that purpose, not shoehorned into a preexisting private dwelling—slowly emerged. Yet there was a big difference between sharing my home with the community and the new kind of house I imagined. Had I grasped the degree of difficulty it would take, I might have thrown that out. I began an exciting journey that challenged my obedience to Scripture in ways I never dreamed.

In the meantime, I discovered that my church wanted to sell four acres of their land on Lake Wassermann to cover the expense of a paved parking lot. That crazy idea of purchasing those acres just took on wings. The land included a lake with a creek separating it from the church property and already zoned ministry. Where could I find a more perfect location for my new idea? It was part of a neighborhood on the edge of town a few blocks away from a main highway. It was a rare location for sale at the perfect time and owned by the church I helped establish. Again, I watched the scenario of God's perfect will fall into place before my eyes.

I wrestled for a year about the meaning of being a Steward, knowing it covered my possessions, position, home, goals, family, health—even my failures and successes. "The call is the expression of the nature from which it comes, and we can only record the call if the same nature is in us. The call of God is the expression of God's nature, not our nature."[16] Is creating a new Blessing House a call of God?

One of my favorite poems, "The Road Not Taken," by Robert Frost captures the key question in the life of faith—the question of choice itself. How do we choose to live our lives? Which way do we turn in times of uncertainty and fear? It matters where we turn for guidance. Without the eternal guiding presence of God, there is no basis for choosing one way over another. Frost's poem is a poignant reminder that every road we take requires us to leave another behind.

I found myself confronting the most important choice in my life. I could either choose to give everything back to God or not. Whichever choice I made would determine the future course of my life.

I had accomplished everything I had ever imagined possible: advanced degrees; international travel; redesigning my home and garden rooms; stimulating work with Dr. Don Bierle's apologetics ministry; and creating an environment used by hundreds for teaching, events, and parties. They were all change agents and very fulfilling years.

And now God was suggesting I go back into the "underbrush" where He was waiting to give me my heart's desire. He was inviting me to totally entrust everyone and everything into His hands. Lots of pieces to this puzzle requiring more people, contributions, and complex legalities than I ever imagined. My decision only came with the word He had given me in Second

---

16 Oswald Chambers, *My Utmost for His Highest*, devotional for January 16 (New York: Dodd, Mead & Company, 1935).

Corinthians 15:6–15. I had to take it a verse at a time—believing it against my own self-perspective. Based on those seven verses, I said YES. And here I was looking at my seventh decade with a major change point at hand to finish well.

REFLECTION

"What if you give everything back to Me, I've ever given you?" Was this a special question just for me that early morning? I heard it and it intrigued me. But why? Was there anyone else ready to hear such a question?

Isaiah overheard God asking, "Whom shall I send? And who will go for us?" (Isaiah 6:8, NIV), and to no one in particular. It was a heavenly vision, and Isaiah's lips had been touched with a burning coal to take away his guilt and atone for his sin.

Is this why he had ears to hear? Were my ears ready to hear such a radical question because of the reality of that same gospel?

"For many are called, but few are chosen,"[17] says Jesus. Oswald says this means that "few prove themselves the chosen ones. The chosen ones are those who have come into a relationship with God through Jesus Christ whereby their disposition has been altered and their ears unstopped, and they hear the still small voice questioning all the time, 'Who will go for us?'"[18]

Is this what happened to me? There was no compulsion or pleading—simply a question that hung in the air resonating something within me. Are there others who have been touched

---

17 Matthew 22:14, ESV

18 Oswald Chambers, *My Utmost for His Highest*, devotional for January 14 (New York: Dodd, Mead & Company, 1935).

by such a question? If so, I believe like me they would have previous experiences with a trail of losses that did not defeat them.

To leave behind all ownership of your life, goods, family, position, home, and goals would be impossible without a deep recognition of how easily each of these could be removed and how deeply you recognize that all of you belongs to God.

DISCUSSION

Looking back years later, I began to see my life as a series of change points strung together, moments of crisis when I had to choose which fork in the road to take. At these crossroads, which I call change points, the issue at stake was always clear: I could choose to believe in the truth of Scripture and risk the consequences or turn my back on God and sink into despair. There really was no middle ground.

Once again, I chose to stand on the edge of the unknown by stepping out in faith. But this was the biggest change point of all. This time, I was holding nothing back, trusting God with *everything* I had, putting my whole life in His hands, without knowing exactly what it meant.

1. Identify change points in your life. Can you see how God was at work to direct you?

2. How did they come?

3. How did they change you?

4. What new insights did you gain about God and His ways?

ACTION

I created a timeline on a long piece of paper to physically see my life journey. I included events of the world, presidents, places I had lived or experienced, other people in my life and family affairs. One could include spiritual learnings, encounters, and gifts. I used markers, objects, photos or pictures, or descriptive words to illustrate my life. It was a great learning tool to see how God had worked in my life, and the trial I had left or the path I was on became more real.

It is helpful to physically view your years on the earth with a collection of photos of people and places. Or draw a map of important places, of travel, living places, or dream places. Your story is important, and visuals can instigate memory, feelings, and insights.

CHAPTER THIRTEEN

THE ROAD TAKEN

***"Way stations are important, but they should never be mistaken for the journey's end."*[19]**

KURT BRUNER AND JIM WARE,
FINDING GOD IN THE LORD OF THE RINGS

My heart was speeding forward, but my head kept turning back.

It was May 10, 2012, closing day on the sale of 227 Lakeview Terrace in Waconia, Minnesota, and time to leave my home of the past twenty-eight years. I awoke early that morning after a fitful night's sleep, both looking forward to and tremulous about the change to come. In the last year of prayer and reflection, I'd chosen to trust God with everything I had by giving back to Him

19 Bruner and Ware, *Finding God in the Lord of the Rings*.

all the material possessions I took for granted (2 Corinthians 9:6–15). I was disowning the concept of ownership itself, and today it all became real.

The plan was carefully laid out and affirmed according to Scripture. I'd gained the confidence to know this was the right decision and the next chapter of my life in God's epic story. But knowing something and feeling it are never the same. I'd taken other big risks before in my walk with God, but this was the furthest I'd ever climbed out on a limb. Thankfully, these words echoed in my mind: "'For I know the plans I have for you,' declares the Lord, 'plans to prosper you and not harm you, plans to give you hope and a future'" (Jeremiah 29:11, NIV).

Before driving to the title company to sign the papers and hand over the keys, I stopped by the house for one last look. This last crossing of the threshold proved to be more wrenching than expected. The family history here was soaked in good memories and friendships, and there was only so much preparing one could do for last goodbyes.

Our family had enjoyed some of our best years here after moving to the small town of Waconia, Minnesota, twenty-five miles west of downtown Minneapolis. Our lives were never dull. Our three very active boys brought a lot of traffic through the front door from the moment we arrived! We felt warmly welcomed to the neighborhood, and life flowed freely into and out of this house.

From the beginning, our home was a gathering place for others, whether it was a tiny garden-level apartment in Minneapolis, our modest split-entry in Bloomington, or this fifties' rambler on Lake Waconia. Bob and I loved generating an atmosphere where people could relax, be themselves, knowing they were always welcome. It was easy to become active in the social and civic life of the community with the Island View Golf Club becoming a second home to both us and the boys. I served in many leadership positions in our church and was elected to the Waconia School Board twice, besides volunteering in other groups and causes.

It was hope that brought us to Waconia. In Bloomington, the reality of Bob's drinking was becoming more obvious, and something had to change; we needed a fresh start. He blamed the stress and faster-paced life of the Twin Cities for fueling his frustrations. Because he had grown up in a small town, he believed a slower pace of life would bring him peace. Though we didn't know it at the time, Waconia means "fountain" or "spring" in the language of the Dakota Sioux, the area's original inhabitants. Our family certainly needed some refreshing, and in multiple ways, we found it and thrived for many years.

This house of joy and renewal also became a place of grief and loss. Here, I mourned Bob's slow, heartrending decline and death from alcoholism in 1993, and the swift, unexpected death by cancer of my second husband, Jerry Stangret, only eight months after our marriage in 1996. It was here, on September 15, 2001, almost exactly four years from the date of Jerry's death, that I received the heartbreaking phone call from a close friend informing me that my youngest son, Tyson, had died in a motorcycle racing accident. In different ways, the grief and loss following each of these deaths shook me to the core, leading me to major crossroads, change points, where I faced the choice of trusting God when I felt most abandoned by Him.

Like the mythological phoenix rising from the ashes, death was never the end of these stories. The house bore witness to redemption and resurrection. The blessings I received through obedience to the Word in these times of greatest trial became a door into a world of ever-expanding dimensions.

God's travel plan from our home in Waconia to the Blessing House in Victoria, Minnesota, was not the shortest, straightest, or smoothest. The contract was signed to purchase four acres from Waterbrooke Community Fellowship, and a highly rated architect-builder was contracted to both design and build this new concept of a house. But a lot of groundwork had to be done before the bulldozers could move in. The church and friends prepared the property with prayer and the anointing of the four corners. All the surveys were still to be completed, and the land needed to be marked with a big sign: "The Future Home of the Blessing House."

Even before that the required legal matters of a nonprofit took many months, and the meetings with the city, county, and state were ongoing. And that came only after a year of documentation of the purpose and mission of the Blessing House, the gathering of support, and the bringing together of a board of directors, the most important piece of the puzzle.

The men and women who were called to this project had talent, expertise, and backgrounds in buildings, finance, entrepreneurship, and marketing. Those who were inspired to offer their services believed this project as ordained by God and took personal responsibility to bring it to pass. This was the backbone of the project.

With the leadership unified in mind and purpose, the Blessing House survived many challenges of establishing a new kind of ministry. Without the wealth of knowledge and commitment of the board, this project would never have been completed. The big movers and dozers bullied the land until the culvert, the road, and the grading were done. Church volunteers cleaned the bog of all the debris left over the years. Ten men requested permission to prayer walk over the project as the Lord directed. That fall they completed their mission, the foundation was poured, and the concrete walls put in place.

As I walked the base, anointing the foundation of the Blessing House with the Oil of Joy, I confirmed that here the material and the spiritual world were joined together. I remembered the groundbreaking celebration with the Waterbrooke congregation, the board of directors, my family, and the architects all in one place celebrating what the Lord was doing. Golden shovels, balloons, speeches, songs, and prayers all celebrated the vision of the Blessing House.

Before a single sketch was made, I shared my vision of the project with the architect and his team. We met in Waconia where they measured every piece of furniture to coincide with my perception of the rooms, walked through every area, photographing my ideas, and asking for my philosophy of space. While we were both entering unknown territory, the house on Lakeview Terrace was my inspiration.

"We have never built a blessing house before," he said. The Victoria project would grow from the ground up, each aspect and element of the structure and its relationship to the site organically emerging from deliberate intention and choice. The team visited several times to get a better feel for the way I lived, what I liked, and how I made choices.

Detailed designing began with the question of trade-offs and priorities. I had more ideas and desires than could be accommodated, but the essentials were there to create a structure with spiritual moorings. The vision was not the result of some logical, linear, systematic process; it came to me in bits and pieces revealed over time in reflections, conversations, dreams, and visions.

The process was analogous to staging a theatrical production. I imagined myself as the scriptwriter, director, and prop master all rolled into one. What did I want to see happen in each part of the house? What sets and props would produce the conversations and interactions people needed to become more closely connected to their authentic selves, each other, and God? How did I want people to feel when they entered the various rooms? The details of décor composing a room had to contribute meaning both in themselves and with their surroundings. The intention guiding our choices was to create spaces for God to work in people's lives. The purpose for the high ceilings, grand walls of windows showing the lake, a fireplace set in an old European wall of stone down to the smallest space was to create a flow of memory, energy, and delight.

My approach to designing the children's room is a good example. I wanted them to walk into a story already going on in a little house just their size. They could play on the carpet, sit around their kitchen table, rock baby dolls to sleep, make supper, or build a kingdom with blocks and Tinker toys and logs. Games, movies, art, and stories could be experienced around the fireplace, and always there were suitcases of things to explore. Open shelves, a window to order snacks from the café, and lots of color to enchant their imaginations. Whether it was a toy horse, a ninja warrior, or an airplane, I wanted children to feel called to pick it up and create a story.

All windows overlooked gardens or sunsets, water or mysterious bogs, and inviting paths to follow. Inside and out melded into one glorious space that invited exploration or dreaming and imagining new ideas. Even the front door was part of an outdoor garden room that invited visitors to slow down, smell the roses, sit in the swing, and wait just one more tantalizing moment before walking through the heavy, mysterious door that says, "WELCOME, COME IN!"

That was my dream, but for it to come true, I had one more hurdle to jump, one more setback requiring trust, one more person to stand in the way of the dream. The architect with a fine reputation, a top winner for twenty-five years in designing magnificent homes, was also a fraudulent builder. I discovered the deceit when I heard from my electrical contractor that no one was getting paid, so the house was dangerously close to not being built. Immediately I called the banks, the lawyers, and the board. It was an unsavory story that resulted in the architect and his partner being convicted of fraud and sentenced to time in prison.

I was heartbroken with the loss of another dream slipping through my fingers. It raised serious doubts in my mind about the vision of it all and caused me to question some of the most basic assumptions about myself and God. Had I become overconfident in myself and my abilities, or had I indulged myself in wishful thinking? In my zeal to create, had I naively overlooked the cold, hard facts of the real world? Did I hear God right?

I'd gone through so much of my life feeling confident and then experiencing loss. Of taking risks and being attacked. Looking back, I wondered what gave me that kind of assurance to keep going, to start again, to find a new idea. "What made me think I could do that?" I would ask myself. Maybe I had overstepped this time and taken on more risk than I could handle.

I again found myself challenging God with this one question, "This too?" I was weeping in confusion and defeat as I walked a path around the lake one day, when I suddenly started singing in tongues. When I asked God what I was singing about when I had lost everything and made both Him and me look foolish, He answered with, "You are singing about my faithfulness! And as those geese flying overhead will return in the spring, so will this house be built."

My son Ryan had taken the lead in collecting the evidence of fraud and taking it to the Minnesota Commerce Department, who then ordered the court to hear the case that involved ten families other than ours. My sons respected my firm decision to not bring charges against a Christian brother, even though he was eventually convicted. We would not begin the life of the Blessing House in the court system. Ryan now brought in a new builder, and with his brother, Kyle, arranged the financial picture to cover the losses. Their leadership and conviction about the Blessing House project brought everyone together, and the construction zone was again humming.

I had planned on celebrating my seventieth birthday in the new building but recognized that would not be possible. Ryan and his wife, Nancy, picked me up for an evening meal with the whole family, and as we drove by the construction, I saw a light on. Ryan said we should check it out. To my total astonishment, the house was lit up with candles, all the building debris had been swept away and replaced with white-covered tables of candles and laden with food and wine. My whole family was there, including brothers and sister, grandchildren, and all my sons' families. It was a Cinderella moment that I will never forget. Never have I felt so loved.

We didn't open on my birthday as planned but opened the doors March 2013 with an enormous celebration. Food and drinks and live music, worship, and testimony abounded. The Blessing House had come true beyond my wildest dreams as the people poured in to see this thing that had come to pass.

REFLECTION

The unexpected challenges, setbacks, and betrayal created a high value to the Blessing House because the enemy did not want this built. We celebrated and praised our God for bringing it to pass, and everyone knew it was the Lord's doing. "Take your hands off this house," I heard the Lord say as I wept through the construction zone. "This is mine and it will be built." How did I know it was the voice of God in my head? Because I would never have come to that conclusion on my own when I surveyed the disaster of the fraud.

There are verses in the Bible that have rescued me from disastrous events in my life that would have defeated me. Galatians 2:20 is the flagship of my life, both in good times and in life-altering times. Knowing I have a life force in me that cannot be defeated energizes me when I have touched bottom. Knowing He who cannot be defeated is the life residing in me grants me an unbeatable spirit.

The fact that I could have lost everything because I trusted a man well-known, documented by my pastor, and successful as a top architect was the last thing I expected. Greater than that reality, however, was the day my son Ryan announced to the board, "This blessing house is going to get built because Kyle and I will see to it. And we will not join the other ten families who are suing." The whole experience took my breath away but strengthened my faith in God's plan and provision, despite the enemy's attempt to destroy it.

DISCUSSION

What is your reaction to the idea of a God-sized calling that is something larger than what you can accomplish within your own power? Remember, I was seventy when I moved into the Blessing House and had never built anything from scratch.

Describe a time when you had a vision (picture, idea) of something you could do that was need-driven, design-driven, or experience-driven. What did you do? What was the result?

ACTION

Knowing who you are in Christ, being ordained by the Father and empowered by His Spirit, will change your life. Here are some verses for you to turn to for life-giving truth:

Ephesians 2:10
1 Peter 2:9–10
Colossians 1:13
Colossians 3:1–4
Hebrews 4:16
1 Corinthians 6:19–20

Continue to journal your dreams because the process sets ideas in place, so you recognize them as God begins to bring resources toward you. Daily Scripture readings will speak to you more personally when there are ideas floating through your head.

CHAPTER FOURTEEN

THE PRACTICAL MYSTIC

"By wisdom a house is built,
and through understanding it is established;
through knowledge its rooms are filled with
rare and beautiful treasures."
(PSALM 24:3–4, NIV)

The halls of the Blessing House are quiet now, a stark contrast to the holiday spirit of the visitors stopping by these past few weeks. Hospitality rings in greetings, introductions, welcomes, the crackling fire, laughter, music, the buzz of conversation, and then a sacred hush, a rest, as folks settle into the beauty of Christmas. The house is happy with these harmonies, both sound and silence welcome the changing seasons.

The excitement and activity that went into planning and hosting fourteen Christmas gatherings, each with its own unique decorative theme, have faded. There are no coats hanging in the guest closet, no piles of shoes and boots lined up by the door. A few small remnants of holiday décor remain, and they too will soon be taken down and whisked back to the storage shelves in the garage from whence they came.

Sitting in the great room by the mammoth stone fireside, wrapped in a blanket, sipping a cup of tea, my body sighs with exhaustion. My breathing slows down as I stare mesmerized into the fire's dancing flames, savoring this long winter's eve.

It is January 6, 2019, the day Christians celebrate Epiphany, when the three wise men arrived to find the newborn lying in a manager. An epiphany is a sudden burst of insight, the clarity that comes from understanding a previously hidden truth. As I look around the Blessing House, I, like the wise men, see the surprising truth that Christ the King wants to be found in humble homes.

Every room in the house contains stories. Around every corner, things burst their material bounds, resounding with the spirit of blessings given and received—tiny clues to the unsolvable mystery left by the Master of the house, the Creator and source of everlasting life. Stories leap off the walls and ceilings, floors, paintings and picture frames, rugs, bookcases, lamps, tables, chairs, coffee mugs, and coasters. Each vignette joins with others as an invitation to linger and enter the story. By some mystical means, the collections of objects harmonize with the invisible realm of spirit, each a thread in a mysterious tapestry woven of spiritual and physical realities. Life here advances against lies, illusions, and self-deception. People are drawn here without knowing why, but often speak of their hearts being touched even as they open the front door. These are subtle keys to the heart's longing for meaning and finding silent satisfaction. A story awaits those who take the time to pause and remember.

Visitors to the Blessing House often say, "I love your art." I used to wonder why because none of it is fancy or expensive. Then I recalled the ways in which these items were selected. Upon entering an antique store, for example, and hearing the little bell on the screen door rattle, I'd get lost in memory, lingering over objects that suggested a story steeped in bygone days. There was a red-checked apron, soft to the touch that smelled of peach pies baked on Saturday mornings at my house. I'd reach for a crock and be transported back to mother's kitchen, with the familiar sounds of dishes rattling. I'd spy an old, framed picture of the Shepherd with His sheep and recall an image of myself sitting around a little table in Sunday School. The smell of color crayons, the dust of sharpened pencils, and the feel of sticky glue on my fingers evoked the sweet presence of the Savior in my life.

As this way of thinking about my relationship to the material world took root, it began altering my day-to-day perceptions and experiences. Combing through thrift stores, garage sales, flea markets, and antique malls, I'd come across some little treasure that made my heart leap, without necessarily knowing why. As the background clutter fell away, I'd feel the comfort, wholeness, and simple quality of beauty emanating from an object. Out of this swirling stew of objects, images, thoughts, and visions, I began to sense a tangible, coherent whole in the merging of matter and spirit. I had no idea what or why this was happening but knew it was for me. I often remarked to the Lord, "I think You are feathering Your nest."

How did I get here? What purpose do I serve? Walking through these now silent rooms, I see my life in panorama—tangible bits and pieces of thoughts, experiences, reminders of family and friends, roads less traveled. I live amidst these artifacts of change and growth, faith and doubt, memories, and associations—tangible manifestations of grief, loss, and redemption. It's all in the mystery of the mundane. In our culture, we rush to the new, the sleek, the magazine look, all of which rarely hold a story. It's easy to outsource the design of a house that reflects current ideals of perfection. It may be beautiful, but it could be anyone's house, or no one's, only a model on a showroom floor. When surveying the interior, does one begin to form a picture of the person living there? Are there clues to the occupant's life story? It's the personal flourishes that reflect the unique identity and character of the occupant.

I know a retired couple who decided it was time to buy a new house just for themselves after raising six children. They found a perfect home as they toured the Parade of Homes and decided to purchase it with all its beautiful contents. A year later, they sold it and bought another home they filled with their personal choices, hung their photos and paintings, and rested among their own memories. They realized that beauty is not a product of perfection but of the unique, the imperfect, the homemade.

I didn't buy something because it was pretty but because my heart had already placed them in my story. There was a flash of recognition in each object, something that reflected an essential part of me. It wasn't an intellectual or abstract experience but a felt connection between the realms of matter and spirit, a juxtaposition of elements pulsing with mystery, beauty, and the energy of rooted, unchanging power.

I can't say exactly where the Blessing House leaves off and I begin. We are two of a kind, perhaps mirrors of each other's space and place, soul and spirit, head and heart, thin places where the seen and unseen touch. The Blessing House sails on uncharted seas. In our fast-changing world, where the illusion of permanence is so relentlessly revealed, can it find sure footing, be a beacon that never flickers?

I would like to be a woman of intelligence who integrates her life and message, reconciles joy and sorrow, but even in this magical, enchanted place, it's easy to get lost and disconnected living between two worlds.

I like to pretend I am living here—which I physically am as I pass through the halls and spaces arranged for others to visit. I live here in a world created with all the things I love to touch and feel and gaze upon—yet I rarely get a chance to sit in it away from my routine normal life as others do. It is a living storybook with characters that appear and disappear in both my real world and that of my imagination. What would it be like if I truly lived in this story rather than arranging it? (journal)

Each new year is a cyclical reminder that our lives are always changing. We never know how the next chapter will unfold. Our minds, bodies, and spirits are constantly in flux, shifting undetected from one state of being to another, always becoming a slightly different version of ourselves. I've personally witnessed the results of individuals coming alive after years, even decades, of stumbling in chaos and confusion; people grieving lost or damaged relationships, drawing life-giving solace hidden deeper than the wells of grief and loss; the sick and wounded, in body, mind, and spirit, healed, with the Holy Spirit stirring new hope.

I find myself reflecting on the past year, how I've changed, the direction my life has taken, and wondering what surprises this next year may hold. Here is a heavenly paradox: the God who never changes calls us to be change makers, to step out in confidence and courage to face the Unknown.

It's *just* a house and it's *not* just a house. Therein lies the mystery behind the story of the Blessing House, a living, breathing manifestation of the paradoxical connection between the material and the spiritual. The Blessing House is more than a material structure; it's a composition, the incarnation of a tale whose pages tell the story of countless challenges and the blessings received and its fullness and abundance I have sought to pass on to others. The life of the Blessing House tells a story in a way that words cannot. As I write this book, I am seeing the threads that wove this story together like the tangled back of a complex needlepoint, the hidden, knotted underside from which the beauty on the front is woven.

It's getting late, time for bed. I pick up my things, turn off the lights, and put things back where they belong. I find myself gravitating toward the long, empty dining table, where twelve chairs are neatly tucked under. Looking out the floor-to-ceiling windows, the waters of Lake Wassermann glimmer in the moonlight. I am in awe and contained in the silent ways of God.

I love the house at midnight
With snow simply falling.
And the moon providing
Quietude from life.
Without a word, I tiptoe round
A child exploring night.
All is bathed in wonder
At the majesty of sight,
Within, around, upon
A house built as a blessing.
The heartbeat of the Lord is here
The breath of life a sound
That sings as music of the spheres
Unheard by human ears
Except at midnight in the moonlight
From angelic realms
That gathers notes from many years
And blends them into song.
Memories of long ago
And movement through the years
Guide my eyes as they alight on
Treasures found tonight.
Stories rise on waves of tears
Soundless, as is right
To keep the silence as I wander

Through the midnight sites.
God has made a house of me
A temple to his liking
Where He is free to roam within
And rest in his abiding.
—GAIL BERGER

REFLECTION

My day usually starts at sunrise, awakened by the chirping of birds—not outside my window, but on a CD of bird sounds. The chirping is a comforting and familiar sound of my childhood. I wrap myself in a blanket, wander into the parlor and sit on the couch. I keep a variety of books close at hand, from which I wander through to feed my soul.

The beauty and wonder of nature put me in a frame of mind to appreciate the simple joys of life. In our day it's easy to lose sight of the miraculous world of our everyday lives. There's precious little time for wandering and wondering even in our homes, which are often driven by the infernal speed of computers and other idols of speed and efficiency. We are a demanding species. We want what we want when we want it but don't realize the cost of speed. Rarely are we deeply challenged to weigh our *wants* against our *needs*. Nature never rushes to do anything. It abides in its own time, patiently unfolding the miracle of existence in ways beyond our comprehension. The Blessing House's greatest value to its guests is its invitation to slow down.

DISCUSSION

How do you create spaces for slowing down, for staring into space, for conversations? Books, blankets, good light, windows, art, a place for your special drink? Beautiful view?

Because I have *zoe*, I see myself as an eternal one walking in time and space. Therefore, I can relax because I have all the time I need to complete God's plan for me. Read Second Corinthians 9:6–15. In the light of this passage, how would you answer this question: What if I had all the time (*zoe*) I need to complete God's plan for me?

ACTION

Take time to sit in every chair and look at what you see...is it pleasant? Inspiring? Inviting?

Cut out pictures from magazines for inspiration and keep files of ideas, so when you see an item, you already know where it fits. When you look at a magazine, identify what you like in the pictures. What appeals to you? It could be the window, the arrangement of items or furniture, the color scheme.

Here's what I did. I sat in every chair in my house, laid in every bed and looked at what others would see. I noted where something needed color or beauty. I changed the direction of the couch or something that was on the wall, so that every place I sat or looked, I could see something beautiful or pleasing.

EPILOGUE

HOPE OF GLORY

In 2019, I spent a week at the Seagull House, a beautiful Frank Lloyd Wright-inspired home in Northern Minnesota on the shores of Lake Superior. I needed to free myself from the daily responsibilities and distractions of running the Blessing House so I could focus on this book. Months earlier, my nephew and owner of the Seagull House, Larry Berger, had kindly invited me to spend a week writing and reflecting in this sublime setting. I booked a week in early October.

During the five-hour drive to northern Minnesota, I had time to ponder all the contradictory emotions I felt when the fraud and deception swirling around the Blessing House's construction came to light. How often conflicting emotions of joy and grief, confusion and revelation, doubt and faith have intermingled in my spiritual life. I also recalled that only by expanding my perspective to include God's hand in my life helped me through to the other side of difficulties.

I reached my destination a little before dusk greeted by the sound of an angry sea of ten-foot whitecaps battering the rocky shore. Yet inside the house, the low-lit warmth of wood and stone welcomed me with a calm and comforting atmosphere—a stark contrast to the tempest outside. Wearied by exhausting events of the past several weeks, I melted into the arms of a beautifully ordered home. It took several days of rest before I was able to focus on the book.

Though I'd begun the writing in November 2018, and ambitiously planned to finish within the year, a series of setbacks and delays at the Blessing House had pushed back the timeline. I wanted the book ready to send my friend and director of the C. S. Lewis Institute in time for the Institute's upcoming triennial conference in July 2020.

This setback is a pattern in my life. Just as I begin to make progress toward some important goal, my plans are thwarted by life events over which I have no control and my dreams of success snatched away. As I settled into the Seagull House that first night and slowly recharged my batteries, I recalled the story of "The Little Bamboo Tree" that helped me navigate confusing times.

The story was told to me by Clara Jones, a lovely eighty-year-old woman who became one of the delights of my life. I had heard stories about her from the Berger family, who lived across the street from her tiny house in Erskine, Minnesota, the small town where Bob grew up.

I didn't know quite what to expect the first time I knocked on her quaint little door. Based on her reputation, I had pictured someone larger than life. Instead, I was greeted by a tiny woman in a tiny house in that tiny northern Minnesota town. Instinctively I knew, however, there was nothing insignificant about Clara's life and mission.

"Ach, Gail," she said with her thick Norwegian accent. "Come in. We'll have tea and talk about Yessus."

That was her greeting every time we met for tea. Still sharp-witted and energetic, she'd developed a Bible study and was teaching a small group in her home about the End Times, rare in those small communities.

The more I learned about her life on those delightful visits, the more entranced I became by the epic nature of her story. As a ten-year-old, Clara knew that someday she was going to China as a missionary. Years later as an adult, her vision came true. She left home expecting to apply her advanced education as a teacher on the China mainland. Yet history interfered, and her first seven years in China coincided with the onset of the Cultural Revolution, those seven bloody years of political oppression during which Mao Tse-Tung rooted out dissenters and ruthlessly persecuted Christians.

Instead of a classroom, Clara spent those seven years living with the Chinese people under horrendous conditions. Constantly on the run, walking through muddy, flooded fields, sleeping in makeshift tents, her life was focused on escaping torture and execution at the hands of Mao's soldiers. When she asked why, the Lord said, "I want you to know my people."

Following the war, she lived in Hong Kong, where she spent many years teaching at a university and often stood up for Christ in debates with other leaders to packed auditoriums. At the time of our first meeting, she kept in touch by mail with some of her former students who attended her Christian classes and now held positions in the Hong Kong government.

At one point, I showed up at her door feeling distraught and discouraged. Clara didn't offer advice or tell me what to do but instead poured me a cup of tea, sat down across the table, and in her wise and loving way proceeded to tell me a story about a bamboo tree. While it takes place in China, variations exist in many cultures, suggesting the universality of its themes.

Clara's story of the Little Bamboo Tree shed new light on my situation, and the lesson has stayed with me ever since. No matter what gets stripped away in life, no matter how painful the paring-away process feels, God can always redeem our suffering—if we let Him. There's no way to predict how or when it will be redeemed, only that His timing is perfect. From the eternal perspective, no experience, no matter how seemingly insignificant or unnecessary, is ever wasted. Though Clara saw the Church and many Christians literally cut to pieces during her years in China, she also saw the power of God's Word flow through their brokenness. The cut-down bamboo tree didn't live to see the blessings of life it bestowed on all those other bamboo trees. For good or ill, we rarely witness all the ripple effects of our words and deeds on others.

So often in my own life, and in the story of the Blessing House, I had the rug pulled out from under me when least expected. At such times, when all seemed lost and the certainty of my identity and purpose swept away, I floundered on a sea of uncertainty. Yet even in the darkest times, I've witnessed the life-giving power of Scripture and God's infinite redeeming love. God has used each loss in my life to strengthen the power of His life of patience, faith, and fortitude. In the process, He strengthened the foundation of the Blessing House inside me and opened its doors ever wider to the world.

Clara was in her mid-nineties and living at an assisted living center the last time we met. By then, her memory was shaky on some things but crystal clear on others. On entering the dining room, I saw this diminutive woman wrapped in a blanket sitting in her wheelchair.

"It's Gail," I said, approaching her. "Do you remember me?"

"Oh, no," she said.

"That's okay," I said. "Tell me what you've been thinking about lately, Clara."

"Well," she said, "I've been thinking that across that dining room wall, we should hang a banner with big letters: "Christ Jesus, Your Hope of Glory."

I want to be like that when I turn ninety!

I returned home from my writing retreat with a renewed sense of hope and trust that nothing done in love is ever wasted or in vain. It's the story of the cross—life resurrected in a new way. Out of the body and blood of Jesus, the words on Clara's banner—"Christ Jesus, Your Hope of Glory"—brought me back to life.

We have been looking at key change points in my life that led me to open the door to a blessing house. A blessing house is not an inanimate thing, but an embodiment, the incarnation of the love of God in your life and the gifts, talents, and resources you receive and return to the Lord for His use. In my case, God's life manifested itself in the material and outward form of a house.

I have also encouraged you to turn anything and anyplace that holds your heart into a blessing for others. Remember, the specific ways you bless your world must come from your own, unique individual life experience God has given you. A true blessing house is not made of bricks and mortar but the blessings inside *YOU*!

As you come to the end of this book, you may be encouraged and inspired or frustrated and confused. These responses and everything in between are perfectly natural and normal. Your blessing house may be an apartment, a house, bedroom, backyard, or not even a place at all, but a talent or an act of service. How you manifest the blessings you've received in the material world can only come from inside you.

No blessing house or story lasts forever; like us, each is mortal, subject to the limits of time and space. All have a beginning, middle, and end. The first form your blessing house takes may not be the last. Each chapter in its story is a living thing and as such will grow, change, and eventually die until a new version springs from your role in God's divine epic. Let the light of Scripture and the Holy Spirit be your guide. Whatever form your blessing house takes, may each who enters your presence be refreshed by the supernatural joy that God alone supplies.

RESOURCES FOR ESTABLISHING THE MINISTRY OF A BLESSING HOUSE

PREPARING FOR CHANGE

Walking in This World: The Practical Art of Creativity by Julia Cameron (Penguin Putnam Inc., 2002)

Live Your Calling: A Practical Guild to Finding and Fulfilling Your Mission in Life by Kevin Brennfleck and Kay Marie Brennfleck (Jossey-Bass)

Defining Moments: How God Shapes Our Character Through Crisis by Rick Ezell (Intervarsity Press, 2001)

To Be Told: God Invites You to Coauthor Your Future by Dan B. Allender, PhD (Waterbrook Press, 2005)

CHANGE POINTS

From Stewardship to Steward: A Theology of Life in All Its Fullness by R. Scott Rodin (Intervarsity Press, 2000)

Money, Possessions and Eternity by Randy Alcorn (Tyndale House Publishers, 1989, 2003)

Stewardship Study Bible, NIV (1972,1978,1984, New International Bible Society)

PRACTICAL WISDOM

The Gospel According to Starbucks: Living with a Grande Passion by Leonard Sweet (Waterbrook Press, 2007)

The Gospel Comes with a House Key: Practicing Radical Hospitality in Our Post-Christian World by Rosario Butterfield (Crossway: 2018)

The Secret Thoughts of an Unlikely Convert: An English Professor's Journey into Christian Faith, by Rosario Champagne Butterfield (Crown & Covenant, 2014)

The Power of Hospitality: An Open Heart, Open Home Will Change Your World, by Chuck & Kathie Crismier (Elijah Books, 2005)

The Limits of Hospitality by Jessica Wrobleski (Liturgical Press, St. John's Abbey, 2012)

ABOUT THE AUTHOR

Gail Berger is the founder and designer of the Blessing House in Victoria, Minnesota. She opened the Blessing House in 2013. Prior to that she used her private residence in Waconia, Minnesota, as the first Blessing House for over fifteen years.

Gail earned a bachelor of arts from Valparaiso University and a master of divinity from Luther Seminary in St. Paul, Minnesota. She served youth as a public school teacher and board member, along with being a youth group leader and Christian education director for her local church. She also has served as a teacher, visitation pastor, and music minister with the residents at her local Good Samaritan Home.

As a pastor, Gail served as an apologist with Dr. Don Bierle's Faith Search Inc. Later she joined Women of God on mission trips to Turkey, Israel, Kenya, Tanzania, and the Philippine Islands. In India, she served as teacher and pastor with Operation Mobilization to the untouchables.

Hospitality, the brotherly love of a stranger, is at the center of Gail's Christian faith. The Blessing House sits on four acres on Lake Wasserman. Individuals, churches, schools, businesses, families, and teaching groups make use of this Christ-centered welcoming home with garden rooms and many spaces all prepared for God to work His wonders.

CPSIA information can be obtained
at www.ICGtesting.com
Printed in the USA
LVHW050205090623
749332LV00008B/498